The 24-Hour Romantasy with ChatGPT

Andrew Parry

Published by Andrew Parry, 2025.

THE 24-HOUR ROMANTASY WITH CHATGPT

First edition. May 4, 2025.

ISBN: 979-8231627806

Written by Andrew Parry.

Table of Contents

Welcome to the World of Romantasy

There's a certain kind of magic that happens when love and fantasy collide. It's not just dragons and kisses or sword fights followed by stolen glances under moonlight. It's about two hearts caught in a world that isn't quite our own, where love grows through trials of fate, ancient curses, political intrigue, and epic quests. Welcome to the world of *Romantasy*—the genre where romance and fantasy hold hands and leap into the unknown together.

Before we dive into how to write one of these beauties in a single day using ChatGPT, let's get clear about what makes Romantasy its own unique experience. It isn't just romance with a fantasy backdrop. And it isn't fantasy with a little flirtation thrown in. It's something much deeper. In a true Romantasy story, the love story is just as important as the fantasy plot—and the fantasy plot is often what makes the romance even more meaningful.

Imagine two enemies from rival magical kingdoms forced to work together on a quest to save their world. Or a lone mage whose heart is guarded more tightly than her powers, until she meets someone who can speak to both. Or maybe it's a story of a healer and a cursed immortal, each searching for freedom, only to find each other instead. These are the kinds of tales readers come to Romantasy for—love stories woven through enchanted forests, moonlit battlefields, or floating cities where the stars themselves whisper secrets.

Romantasy is wildly popular right now, and not just with readers. Writers are diving into this genre because it lets you blend emotion and imagination in the most satisfying ways. It's world-building meets heart-building. You get to create new rules for magic, societies, and destinies, and at the same time you're crafting a story about two people falling in love—usually against impossible odds.

But here's the fun part: with tools like ChatGPT, you don't have to go it alone. Writing a Romantasy used to take months of mapping, plotting, and waiting for inspiration to strike. But now, you can have a creative partner who helps you brainstorm ideas, structure your plot, design your world, and even rewrite your scenes when they feel flat. You're still the boss, still the storyteller, but now you've got someone who never runs out of energy or ideas to bounce off of.

Think of ChatGPT like your enchanted writing quill. You bring your heart and vision to the table, and it helps you shape it into something structured and stunning. You can ask it for names of magical towns, or descriptions of a lover's eyes that read like poetry. You can say, "Write a scene where the heroine has to choose between her love and saving the world," and it'll give you three versions before you even finish your coffee. You don't have to use everything it gives you—but what it does is *move you forward.* And in a one-day writing sprint, that's exactly what you need.

Let's also acknowledge something up front: writing a full story in one day doesn't mean you're rushing or cutting corners. It means you're focusing. You're committing to the emotional truth of your idea, and you're letting the words flow without fear. ChatGPT helps eliminate that second-guessing voice in your head that says "this isn't good enough." It lets you play. Explore. Say yes to scenes you'd otherwise abandon. The time pressure actually makes you more instinctual—and Romantasy is a genre that thrives on intuition and emotion.

Before we go further, take a moment and ask yourself this: *What do I want my Romantasy to feel like?* Do you want it to be sweeping and tragic, like a star-crossed fate? Do you want it to be playful and sweet, like a magical rom-com in a pixie forest? Do you want it to be steamy, mysterious, cozy, dark, hopeful, tragic, fierce? All of these are valid—and your vibe will shape the kind of world you build and the kind of characters who live in it. ChatGPT can help you refine that tone and even suggest scenes or dialogue that match it, but you need to be clear with yourself about what kind of emotional ride you want to take your readers on.

One thing that makes Romantasy different from straight romance or fantasy is that you need to be constantly balancing two arcs. There's the external story—what's happening in the world. The danger, the quest, the magic system, the politics. And there's the internal story—the emotional arc between the main couple. How they change because of each other, how they come together, fall apart, fight for love, and earn their happy (or tragic) ending.

The two arcs need to feed each other. That means your fantasy elements can't be disconnected from the romance. If your heroine is a cursed knight, maybe only her true love can break the curse. If your world is on the brink of collapse, maybe love is the only thing strong enough to save it—or worth saving at all. Romantasy is most satisfying when the fantasy *and* the romance feel necessary to each other.

Now, in this book, we're going to take you step-by-step through writing your Romantasy story or short novel in just one day. You'll learn how to:

- Use prompts and templates with ChatGPT to instantly generate story structure ideas
- Create characters with rich emotional depth and compelling motivations
- Build fantasy worlds that are vivid, fresh, and totally yours
- Explore romantic tropes and how to subvert or elevate them
- Map out your entire story quickly so you don't waste time figuring it out mid-chapter
- Write emotional and magical scenes that stick in the reader's heart
- Keep your writing flowing even when you feel stuck, using ChatGPT as a guide

By the end of this journey, you'll have a complete Romantasy draft that you can polish later—or even publish if it's ready. This is your story, your world, and your love story to bring to life.

And if you've never written anything before, don't worry. That's the magic of this approach. You're not required to be an expert in world-building, or know the difference between plot beats and pacing arcs. You just need a spark of an idea and the willingness to follow where it leads. ChatGPT will help you build the structure around that spark.

So what's next? In the following chapters, we'll look at how to turn that flicker of an idea into something you can hold, read, and even share with the world. You'll learn how to trust your instincts, how to dance with the rhythm of your imagination, and how to use AI not as a crutch, but as a creative co-pilot.

Romantasy is about love—and writing one should feel like falling in love with your story. That's what today is about. One day. One story. One magical adventure.

Ready to begin?

Why ChatGPT is the Writing Partner You Didn't Know You Needed

Let's start by being real. Writing can be lonely. Sometimes beautifully so, but often frustratingly so. You sit down with an idea burning in your chest, only to stare at a blank page for hours, unsure how to shape it into anything real. You might have the start of something—a character, a scene, a feeling—but getting from there to an actual story? That's where a lot of writers get stuck. This is where ChatGPT swoops in like a literary sidekick with a bottomless imagination and zero judgment.

Now, maybe you've heard people say AI writing tools are only good for drafting boring marketing emails or robotic blog posts. But that's because they haven't learned how to dance with one. ChatGPT isn't here to write the story *for* you—it's here to help you write it *with* more joy, speed, and surprise than you thought possible. If you're open to collaboration, this tool becomes a kind of mirror, muse, editor, and engine all rolled into one.

In Romantasy, where feelings run high and worldbuilding runs deep, ChatGPT can be the bridge between what's in your heart and what ends up on the page. Think of it as a creative companion who's available 24/7, never gets tired, and always has a few fresh ideas up its sleeve. It doesn't replace your creativity—it enhances it. And when you're trying to write a full Romantasy story in a single day, speed and support are everything.

Let's say you've got the seed of an idea: A rogue princess with ice powers is being hunted by a fire-wielding bounty hunter—and somehow, they fall in love. That's a great start. But what comes next? What does the world look like? What's the emotional arc of their romance? What breaks them apart? What binds them together? This is the kind of story that could take weeks to build from scratch. With ChatGPT, you can feed it your idea and get back possible story outlines, full scenes, dialogue snippets, and worldbuilding prompts within minutes. You're not locked into anything—it's like brainstorming with someone who always has time for you and never runs out of fuel.

More importantly, ChatGPT helps you *keep moving*. One of the hardest parts of writing is that little voice in your head that says, "This isn't good enough" or "I don't know what to write next." ChatGPT doesn't hear that voice. It's not worried about perfection—it's focused on possibilities. It keeps the story rolling while you stay in the flow. And honestly, flow is everything in a one-day write-a-thon. You can't afford to agonize over every comma. You need momentum. ChatGPT gives you that.

It also gives you options. Not sure how your lovers should first meet? Ask ChatGPT for three different meet-cutes—one dramatic, one comedic, and one tender. Trying to name a magical city or a forgotten goddess? Ask it for a list of names and meanings. Need help writing that big emotional confrontation scene where one character is about to leave forever? You can generate multiple versions until one hits your heart just right.

One of the best ways to use ChatGPT in writing Romantasy is to treat it like a very fast, very obedient writing room. You're still the showrunner. You decide what's in and what's out. But the moment you need input, it's right there. You don't have to wait for feedback from beta readers or wonder if a scene is working—you can ask ChatGPT to simulate the reader experience and tell you how it feels emotionally, or suggest how to raise the stakes.

The more specific and emotionally honest you are with your prompts, the better it performs. Don't just say, "Write a kissing scene." Say, "Write a scene where a warrior who doesn't believe he deserves love kisses the healer who's risked everything for him, but the world is about to end." Now you're feeding it *emotion*, *stakes*, and *context*. That's when the magic happens. ChatGPT will take that and give you something that may surprise you, move you, or at least get you closer to where you need to go.

Here's another secret: ChatGPT doesn't just help when you're stuck. It's also great when you're flying. Let's say you're in a zone and you've just written a killer scene. You can ask ChatGPT to read it back to you in a different voice, or rephrase it more poetically, or suggest how to expand the emotional beats without dragging the pace. You're not replacing your writing—you're refining it faster, better, and without losing the heat of inspiration.

And the best part? There's no ego in the room. You can throw out the weirdest ideas, take bold risks, and never feel judged. You're free to explore the story in all directions. Want to see what happens if your love interest turns villain halfway through? Try it. Want to write a version where the dragon is secretly in love with the heroine? Go for it. ChatGPT doesn't flinch at plot twists—it leans into them.

For Romantasy, where emotions and imagination intertwine, that freedom is everything. You can use the tool to push deeper into character emotions, sharpen the romantic tension, or stretch your worldbuilding further than you thought possible. It lets you be wild, which is the whole point of writing a story where love defies rules and magic changes everything.

There's also something special about the *speed*. When you commit to writing a full Romantasy in a day, there's no time to get bogged down in perfectionism. You need to move from idea to outline to scenes to climax without hesitation. ChatGPT makes that possible by filling in the blanks and catching you when you start to stall. The faster you go, the more you realize how often writing is about decision-making—and ChatGPT helps you make those decisions faster, with fewer regrets.

Let's be clear: you're still the soul of the story. The heart, the voice, the emotion—that's yours. ChatGPT can help you find the shape of the tale, but it's your passion and point of view that makes the story worth telling. Think of it like a magical sword in your hand. The weapon is sharp and strong, but only you decide what to fight for, what to protect, and what to say in the end.

So if you've been curious, skeptical, or maybe a little intimidated by the idea of using AI to write fiction—especially a genre as emotionally rich as Romantasy—let this chapter be your permission slip to give it a real try. It's not cheating. It's not lazy. It's not soulless. It's *collaborative storytelling* in a new era.

And when your goal is to create an entire Romantasy story in a single day, you want every tool in your arsenal to be enchanted.

What Is Romantasy Really About? Love, Magic, and Meaning

Romantasy is more than just two genres smashed together for fun. It's not a romance novel in costume or a fantasy story with a little kissing thrown in. Romantasy, when done right, is about love and magic working together to say something deeper—about connection, transformation, sacrifice, destiny, power, and hope. It's a genre with the emotional pull of a love story and the grand sweep of an epic. And when it really sings, it leaves readers not just breathless from the adventure, but emotionally altered by what the characters have gone through.

At its heart, Romantasy is built on dual engines: romance and fantasy. But it's the way they interact that makes it special. It's not just about telling two stories at once—it's about telling one story that couldn't exist without both of those elements holding it up. The love story is strengthened by the stakes and world of the fantasy. The fantasy is made more human, more tender, more immediate by the presence of the romance. They work in tandem, not parallel.

Think of it this way: in a pure romance, the central tension is emotional and interpersonal. It's about two people navigating their internal baggage, external pressures, and the unpredictable chemistry between them. In a traditional fantasy, the tension is often epic and external—saving the world, mastering magic, toppling empires, facing destiny. In Romantasy, those two tracks collide. Suddenly, the fate of a kingdom might rest on whether two soulmates can trust each other. Or a magical war might be the metaphor for the walls someone's built around their heart. Every external battle reflects an internal one, and vice versa.

What makes Romantasy even more gripping is that it's not bound by realism. You're free to use metaphor as literal truth. A character carrying emotional scars might also literally wear runes etched into their skin. A romance torn apart by betrayal might be mirrored by a shattered magical relic they once used together. You're allowed—and encouraged—to be symbolic, poetic, and mythic, because Romantasy readers aren't just tolerating the magic, they're *hungry* for it. They want the romance to feel like fate and the world to feel like legend. They want their hearts broken and rebuilt inside a place that could only exist on the page.

But none of this works unless the emotions are real. That's where a lot of fantasy stories that *try* to be Romantasy fall flat. They focus so much on the worldbuilding—the rules of magic, the factions, the lore—that the romance ends up feeling like a side dish. Readers can tell. Romantasy fans want to *feel* the slow burn, the longing, the heartbreak, the euphoria. If the romance isn't central—if it doesn't grow and challenge the characters the way the plot does—it doesn't land.

So what is Romantasy really about? Let's break it down into three key ideas: **love, magic, and meaning**. Not just the presence of those things, but the *interaction* between them.

Love, in Romantasy, is usually forbidden, complicated, or fated. Rarely is it simple or easy. And that's the point. The genre thrives on the idea that love is worth fighting for—not just against societal norms, but against monsters, curses, destinies, and inner demons. The lovers aren't just trying to be together; they're trying to *become* the kind of people who *can* be together. That transformation is part of what makes the story feel epic. Romantasy love changes people. It tests them. It makes them braver, softer, wiser, or sometimes even more dangerous.

Magic, in Romantasy, often mirrors the emotional stakes. It's not just there to be cool or flashy. It has rules, sure—but it should also have *resonance*. Maybe the magic is tied to memory, and your character can only cast spells when they're emotionally vulnerable. Maybe a character's power grows stronger when they're in love—or more unstable. Maybe there's a magical bond between lovers, but it makes them feel each other's pain. The magic becomes part of the emotional story, not just the plot. That's when it feels alive.

And then there's **meaning**. This is the thread that ties everything together. Romantasy, at its core, is about finding meaning in the chaos. What does love *mean* in a world on fire? What does sacrifice mean when your heart is on the line? What does it mean to be chosen—not just by destiny, but by someone who sees your worst self and loves you anyway? These are the questions Romantasy dares to ask. And they're the ones readers remember long after they've closed the book.

A good Romantasy isn't just about what happens. It's about what *matters*. That's why so many Romantasy stories feel so personal, even when they take place in imaginary kingdoms with flying creatures and ancient magic. The emotions are real. The doubts, the hope, the ache of yearning, the pain of betrayal, the wild, electric joy of being seen—it all hits harder because it's wrapped in metaphor and magnified by fantasy.

So how do you tap into that? How do you write a Romantasy that feels both grounded and grand? You start by honoring both halves of the genre equally. Don't treat the romance like an afterthought. Don't use the fantasy as window dressing. Think about how they reflect and shape each other. Let your world test your lovers. Let your lovers shape the fate of your world.

And then go even deeper. Ask what *you* want to say about love and power, trust and fate, vulnerability and strength. Use your story to explore your own questions, your own fears, your own longings. Romantasy isn't about writing to market. It's about writing from the heart—with the volume turned all the way up.

This is where ChatGPT becomes your secret weapon again. You can use it to test out what kind of Romantasy you want to write. Ask it: "What if I wrote a story where the magic system is based on emotional repression?" Or "Give me ideas for a Romantasy where the two leads have opposing magical philosophies." Or even "Help me design a kingdom where love is outlawed, but magic is not." ChatGPT will give you variations, pathways, and building blocks that you can explore, twist, or discard until something *clicks*. It's like playing in a sandbox made of your own imagination and someone else's curiosity.

Romantasy is also uniquely suited to nonlinear storytelling. You can play with timelines, reincarnations, dreams, past lives, and prophecies. You can create a tale where the present romance is tangled up in a centuries-old curse. Or one where the lovers keep meeting in different worlds. Or one where the romantic climax is a literal battle for the soul. This genre rewards emotional risk and creative courage.

But again, it all comes back to feeling. If your readers don't *feel* the tension, the connection, the heartbreak, and the magic, it won't matter how many cool worldbuilding elements you've packed in. So use ChatGPT to help *refine* your emotion—not replace it. Ask it how a character might react emotionally to a betrayal. Ask it for metaphors that match the tone of your scene. Ask it how to build romantic tension through subtle dialogue or charged silences. Think of it like having a writing partner who never runs out of new ways to say "I love you"—or "I hate that I love you."

Romantasy is more than a trend. It's a timeless genre that gives readers what they crave most: emotional truth in a world where anything is possible. It invites you to dream bigger, feel deeper, and write stories that crack your heart open just a little.

Start with the Ending: Knowing How the Romance and the Journey Resolve

Here's a bit of writing magic that most first-time Romantasy writers don't realize until halfway through their book: the ending is everything. It shapes everything that comes before it. It's the emotional echo that readers carry with them after the final page. And in Romantasy, where the heart and the world are both on the line, the ending isn't just a conclusion—it's a transformation.

That's why I want you to start there. Before you sketch your magical kingdom or name your shapeshifter prince or map out the slow-burn romance between your warlock and your witch, ask yourself one question: *how does it end?*

And I don't mean in a vague, "they fall in love and live happily ever after" kind of way. I mean specifically. *Where* do they end up? *Who* are they by the final chapter? *What has changed* in the world because of their love—or in spite of it? What did it cost them to get there? Did someone have to give up their magic? Did a crown fall into the sea? Did a prophecy get rewritten? Did they have to walk away from each other to save something greater? Or did they fight like hell to be together, against all odds?

When you write with the ending in mind, everything else becomes a kind of guided path toward it. You don't get lost in the middle because you know what you're aiming for. You don't flounder at the climax because you already built the landing. The ending becomes your North Star. It helps you pace the romance. It helps you shape the arc of your characters. It even helps you decide what kind of fantasy world makes the most emotional sense.

Let's talk about the *two arcs* that Romantasy must resolve: the romantic arc and the fantasy arc. These don't always conclude in the same moment, but they usually echo each other. If your romantic ending is full of heartbreak, your fantasy ending probably reflects some kind of sacrifice or loss. If your lovers unite, it often coincides with a magical victory, a prophecy fulfilled, or a kingdom restored. And if you want to get bold—and you should—it's okay for one arc to be bittersweet while the other soars.

There's something powerful about knowing your romantic ending first. Because then, every scene you write becomes a step in that emotional evolution. If your lovers start out as enemies, and you know they'll end up saving the world together—hand in hand, in love—you can plan the subtle shifts, the tension points, the reversals, and the moments of vulnerability that make that transition feel earned. If they're fated mates who must break the bond to defeat an ancient evil, you can build toward that final tearful goodbye with emotional precision. You can write the ache into every chapter before it.

Same goes for your fantasy arc. If you know the world is going to be remade by the end—whether that's a destroyed empire, a magical revolution, or the healing of a broken realm—then you can plant seeds for that from the very beginning. The ending tells you what questions your story must answer, what themes you need to resolve, and what promises you must keep.

Here's where ChatGPT becomes a wildly helpful partner. If you've got even the smallest idea for an ending, you can describe it in a prompt and ask for different ways to build toward it. Say, "My Romantasy ends with the hero choosing love over power. What are some story arcs that would make that moment powerful?" You'll get suggestions for earlier scenes, character dilemmas, even worldbuilding rules that support that moment. It's like reverse-engineering your story from its most emotional payoff.

And if you don't *have* an ending in mind yet, that's okay too. You can start by exploring *how you want the story to make the reader feel.* Do you want them to sob? Smile through tears? Pump their fist in triumph? Sink into a quiet kind of hope? Tell ChatGPT the emotion, and it can suggest types of endings and the kinds of storylines that lead to them. You're not fishing in the dark anymore. You're shaping the story to serve a feeling—and that's one of the most effective ways to write with purpose.

Some of the most beloved Romantasy books stick in our minds *because* of their endings. That final choice. That kiss under the stars. That sacrifice that still hurts to think about. That last line that redefines the whole journey. So don't treat your ending like a reward you discover at the end of the writing process. Treat it like a destination you're carving a road toward. Even if you change your mind halfway through—and you might—you'll still be writing with direction.

Let's also talk about genre expectations for a second. In Romantasy, readers are often looking for one of three emotional landing zones: happily ever after, bittersweet, or full-blown heartbreak. You don't have to pick the most dramatic one to make an impact—but you do need to pick one that *feels honest* to the story you're telling. A Romantasy where love conquers all needs to go all in on the joy. A Romantasy where love is forbidden must explore the emotional cost. A Romantasy where lovers are torn apart by prophecy needs to feel like the world *meant* for that heartbreak. And if you're really brave, maybe you'll write the kind of ending where the reader still isn't sure what to feel—but they *can't stop thinking about it.*

When you know your ending, you can also begin planting emotional echoes. These are little moments, images, or pieces of dialogue that reflect or foreshadow your final chapter. Maybe the lovers argue in Chapter 3 about whether they believe in fate—and the final chapter proves one of them right in the most devastating or beautiful way. Maybe the heroine sees a ruined castle at the beginning and says she could never imagine calling it home—only to rebuild it in the epilogue with the person she's come to love. These moments land harder because they feel inevitable. They make the ending feel *earned.*

One of the best things about Romantasy endings is how *personal* they can be. It's not just about defeating the villain or saving the realm. It's about whether two people can finally say "I love you" without fear. Whether they can let each other in. Whether they're strong enough—together—to face the world, or wise enough to let each other go. And it's about what their love *means* in the context of the world you've built. Is it rebellion? Is it healing? Is it destiny? Or is it something neither of them expected—but exactly what they needed?

Here's a simple exercise to do before you start writing your story: write the final scene first. Or at least a version of it. Let it be messy. Let it be raw. Write the confrontation, the kiss, the goodbye, the spell, the decision. Feel it out. Then you'll know what kind of emotional threads you need to weave backward from. If that's too intimidating, try writing a one-paragraph summary of the last chapter. Then give it to ChatGPT and ask for an outline that gets you there. The machine will do the legwork; you'll do the soul work.

Writing with the end in mind is like mapping a star before the journey begins. It doesn't take away the surprises—it just gives you the confidence that no matter how wild the middle gets, you know where you're going to land. And when you're writing a full Romantasy story in a day, that kind of anchor keeps you from drifting too far off course.

In the next chapter, we'll go from endings to beginnings—starting with the seed of your Romantasy idea and nurturing it into something big, bold, and bursting with potential. Because once you know where you're going, it's time to figure out *how* to get there.

And it all starts with the spark.

From Idea Spark to Story Concept: Getting Your Romantasy Rolling

Every story starts with a spark. It might be a single image that flashes through your mind—like a girl with silver eyes standing in the middle of a snowstorm, or a knight kissing the enemy prince beneath a blood moon. It might be a line of dialogue you can't stop hearing, or just a vague feeling, like yearning, or destiny, or betrayal. Whatever that first spark is, it matters. It's the first flicker of magic that wants to become something more. But to turn that spark into a Romantasy, you have to give it shape. And that's where we begin turning your emotional idea into a story concept you can write in a single day.

Let's start by acknowledging that not every spark is a plot. That's okay. It doesn't have to be. The story doesn't have to arrive fully formed with three acts and a detailed world already in place. It just needs to *want to live*. Your job is to feed it. Grow it. And use tools like ChatGPT to explore the edges of it until something locks in and lights you up.

Say your spark is something simple like "a witch falls in love with a cursed warrior." That's not a story yet, but it's a delicious start. Now ask yourself a few basic questions to stretch it into something more tangible: Who cursed him? Why is she drawn to him? What kind of magic does she use? What kind of world do they live in? What is at stake—emotionally and magically—if they fall in love?

This is where ChatGPT becomes your partner in creative crime. You can literally take that one-sentence idea and say, "Help me turn this into a full story concept." It will ask the right questions, offer structure, suggest settings, or even propose multiple twists. Suddenly your quiet spark has heat. Direction. Potential. You're no longer staring at a blank page—you're reacting to possibility.

Let's try another example. Maybe your spark is even vaguer: "What if a romance could reshape time itself?" That's juicy. But what does it mean? Is it literal time travel? Is it a magical artifact? Is it a metaphor for breaking a generational curse? Ask ChatGPT, "Give me five story concepts for a Romantasy where love affects time." Watch what comes back. Maybe you'll see something about a time loop that resets every time they kiss. Or a kingdom where every couple is assigned a future prophecy. Or a warlock who can rewind time but only at the cost of forgetting who he loves.

That's how we go from spark to concept. We lean into questions. We follow emotional threads. And we *use* AI to generate options—not because we're lazy, but because we're too smart to waste hours trying to make every creative leap alone. This isn't cheating. This is modern writing. This is collaboration.

Here's a little process that can help you turn your idea spark into a story shape:

Start by identifying three core ingredients:

- The romantic dynamic
- The fantasy element
- The emotional arc

Let's break that down. The romantic dynamic is the core tension between your leads. Are they enemies-to-lovers? Forbidden lovers? Childhood friends reunited under dangerous circumstances? Pick something that excites you emotionally. Not just what's popular, but what makes you *feel* something.

The fantasy element is the magic or worldbuilding twist that makes your story not just a romance, but a Romantasy. It might be magical powers, an alternate world, a kingdom in conflict, a prophecy, a curse, a mythical creature, or a war between realms. Whatever it is, it should do more than look cool—it should tie directly into the emotional stakes of the romance.

And then there's the emotional arc. What do your characters need to overcome inside themselves to be together? This is where the story earns its heart. Is it fear of vulnerability? Guilt from a past mistake? A need to choose duty over desire? The internal arc gives your story depth. Without it, you're just describing events. With it, you're writing a transformation.

Once you have those three things, you've got a seed of a concept. For example:

Romantic Dynamic: Cursed warrior and soft-hearted healer, forced to travel together.

Fantasy Element: A magical forest that warps time, where every path taken changes their past.

Emotional Arc: He believes he's too broken to be loved. She believes no one ever stays.

Story Concept: As they journey through the forest to find a cure, their love begins to rewrite the very memories that haunt them—but changing the past might erase their future.

Boom. That's a story.

You could write that in a day, especially with ChatGPT by your side helping you outline the path, generate scenes, and keep your fingers moving. But the key is that it *started small.* One spark. A flicker of romance and magic. Then curiosity. Then questions. Then shape.

Here's the fun part: you don't even need to land on just one idea at the beginning. You can generate a bunch of rough concepts with ChatGPT, try them out for a paragraph or two, and see what catches fire. You'll know the one. It's the idea you don't want to stop thinking about. The one that makes your chest feel too tight. The one that makes you want to *write right now*.

And if you're worried your idea isn't "original" enough—don't be. There are no new ideas. There are only new *takes.* The most successful Romantasy stories aren't the ones with the most unique worlds. They're the ones with the most emotionally honest characters. What matters is how you tell it. Your voice. Your spin. Your themes. ChatGPT can help you write it fast, but you are the one who makes it real.

This is also a great moment to ask: What do you want this story to say about love? About power? About sacrifice? About choice? About trust? The themes you care about will start shaping the kinds of scenes you write, the kinds of conflicts you create, the kinds of endings you build toward.

So don't be afraid to make your story personal. Maybe your spark comes from something you've felt—grief, longing, betrayal, or that terrifying, fluttering feeling when someone *sees* you. That's gold. Use it. Let it spill into the fantasy. Turn it into magic. That's what Romantasy does—it gives shape to feelings that are too big for reality.

You don't have to know every answer right now. But once you have your concept, you have a path. You can break it into acts, or chapters, or just scenes. You can tell ChatGPT, "Here's my concept—help me outline it." Or "Give me a beat-by-beat breakdown of this story." You're not climbing a mountain alone anymore. You're riding a dragon with a map.

Building a Love Story in a Magical World

Romance and magic. You could try to keep them separate, but where's the fun in that? In Romantasy, these two elements don't just coexist—they dance with each other. They twist around one another like vines, like spells, like fated hands reaching across time. But for that to actually *work* in your story, you need to build a love story that feels emotionally authentic inside a world that is anything but ordinary.

It starts with one simple idea: your romance should be *shaped* by the magical world—not just dropped into it. That means your couple's struggles, connections, choices, and moments of intimacy are all affected by the rules and wonders of the fantasy setting you've created. Maybe magic is forbidden and their bond is dangerous. Maybe they're on opposite sides of a magical war. Maybe love itself has magical consequences—like binding souls, awakening dormant powers, or triggering prophecies. Whatever the mechanic, it's not just background noise. It's part of what makes the romance *feel* alive.

So how do you build a love story in a world that's full of enchanted forests, cursed bloodlines, ancient relics, or magical hierarchies? You start where you always do—with the characters.

Romantasy isn't about people falling in love because the plot says they should. It's about people changing because of the love they find. So ask yourself: what are your characters like when the story starts? Who are they when they fall in love? And who do they become by the end because of it?

This is the emotional heart of the story. Magic might keep them apart, or throw them together, or complicate every decision they make. But the reader is here for *how* these two characters reach each other anyway. How their connection deepens even when everything around them is impossible. They want the tenderness in between the danger. They want the moment one character sees the other's scars—magical or emotional—and chooses to stay.

Now add in the fantasy layer. What about this world makes it harder—or more intense—for them to fall in love? Are there rules against different magical castes mixing? Does one of them have powers that isolate them or mark them as cursed? Are they connected by a prophecy neither of them believes in? Is their romance being manipulated by a god, a spell, or a secret buried in history?

Here's where you get to have real fun. Because every romantic trope—whether it's enemies to lovers, soulmates, forbidden love, or fake dating—gets a fresh coat of magic in a fantasy setting. "Enemies to lovers" becomes two heirs from rival magical dynasties. "Soulmates" becomes a literal soul bond that lets them feel each other's emotions. "Fake dating" turns into a magical ruse to fool a cursed artifact or win over a suspicious court. It's the same emotional beats, but the stakes are higher and the consequences are enchanted.

And let's not forget the *setting* itself. Don't treat your magical world as just a stage. Let it be part of the romance. Where do your lovers steal their moments? What does intimacy look like in a world with floating cities or shadow markets? Is their first kiss under a tree that blooms once a century? Do they dance in a castle that's slowly vanishing from reality? Are they forced to share warmth in a cave made of living crystal? These settings aren't just visual dressing—they *amplify* the emotion. They make every touch, every glance, every near-miss feel like part of something bigger than the characters themselves.

This is also where you can use ChatGPT in wildly creative ways. You can ask it to generate scenes based on very specific moods or magical concepts. Try something like, "Write a romantic scene where a mage and a rogue share a moment of vulnerability inside a library that's alive." Or "Describe a kiss that happens in a world where time slows down when people fall in love." Let the AI flood you with possibilities. Keep what resonates. Shape what sparks something. You'll end up with a love story that's emotionally honest but unlike anything your reader has seen before.

And don't forget emotional progression. A magical world can't shortcut real feelings. Even if your characters are destined for each other or magically bonded, they still have to *choose* love. That's what makes it satisfying. They have to earn each other's trust. They have to grow beyond their flaws. They have to forgive, open up, and risk something real. Love in a Romantasy world still follows the same emotional truths as in any good story—it just does it while riding a dragon.

Let's also talk about *obstacles*. In a regular romance, obstacles might be misunderstandings, past trauma, social class differences, or timing. In Romantasy, you get to add magical barriers that reflect those same emotional hurdles. A character who can't let others in might literally be wrapped in protective magic. A character who feels unworthy of love might be cursed to forget anyone who says they love them. The magic doesn't replace the emotion—it *expresses* it.

And when you're writing fast—when you've only got a day to get from spark to finished story—this layering can actually *help* you move faster. Because you can tie emotional progress to magical changes. When your characters get closer, the magic shifts. When they fight, the environment responds. When they fall in love, the world itself blooms, cracks, or glows. This isn't just a romance inside a fantasy world. It's a romance *that transforms the world.*

Now let's take a moment to think about your lovers at their most connected. What moment in the story will define their love? Not just a kiss, or a confession—but an act. A sacrifice. A promise. Something that says, *I see you, and I choose you—even here, even now, even with everything in ruins.* That moment will be your emotional climax. Everything else will build toward it. And if your magical world is woven tightly enough into your romance, it will feel as epic and mythic as any spell ever cast.

Want to build toward that faster? Ask ChatGPT for help. Try, "What's a Romantasy scene that shows two characters choosing each other over destiny?" or "Give me a moment where love breaks a magical rule." Use the results as fuel. Write fast. Let emotion lead. And don't worry about writing the love story *perfectly.* Just write it *honestly.* Let the characters be messy. Let them make bad choices. Let them struggle to trust. But always, always let them move toward connection—even if the road is painful. That's what Romantasy is about: finding love when the world says you shouldn't. Loving someone who feels impossible. And letting that love matter, not just to them, but to the world they inhabit.

Because in a Romantasy, love isn't just a subplot. It's the force that changes everything.

Finding the Fantasy: What Kind of Magic, Lore, or Creatures Live Here?

The heartbeat of Romantasy isn't just in the romance—it's in the wonder. The kind of wonder that crackles through the air when someone casts a spell, or rises from ancient stones whispering forgotten truths. It's in the strange, haunting beauty of places that don't exist in our world. It's in the creatures, myths, and magics that make readers feel like they've crossed into another realm. If your love story is the soul of your Romantasy, then your fantasy is the body it lives in—and that body needs to be alive, breathing, and just a little dangerous.

Let's make one thing clear from the start: you don't have to invent an entire Tolkien-level mythos to write a great Romantasy. You don't need five different languages, twelve kingdoms, and a fully fleshed-out magical economy. You *can* have all that, sure—but what you really need is something that *feels magical*, something with a few clear rules and a strong aesthetic that serves your story emotionally.

Think about your fantasy elements like set pieces and metaphors. The best fantasy worlds in Romantasy stories are the ones that reflect or amplify the emotional journey of the characters. If your lovers are broken, the world might be shattered. If they're forbidden from being together, maybe magic itself rebels against their union. If one of them is hiding who they truly are, maybe illusion magic plays a major role in the world. The key is to let the fantasy deepen the meaning—not just decorate the background.

So where do you begin? With questions. Not answers—questions. Start asking things like:

What kind of magic exists here?

Where did it come from?

Who controls it?

Is it tied to emotion, to blood, to time, to nature, to ancient gods?

Is it something people are born with, or something they earn—or steal?

Is it beautiful, wild, broken, dangerous?

You don't need to know everything. In fact, a little mystery goes a long way. But you should have *one central idea* about magic that shapes the story. Think of it like a mood ring for your world. Is it soft and dreamlike, with glowing forests and whispering spirits? Or harsh and brutal, with blood rituals and ancient grudges? Choose the tone, then layer in details that reflect that tone.

This is a great time to bring in ChatGPT. Ask it to help you brainstorm magic systems that tie into your story's emotional themes. Try something like, "Give me five magic systems where power is linked to memory and love" or "Describe a fantasy world where falling in love changes how magic works." ChatGPT will spit out frameworks, rules, and aesthetics you can pull from, refine, or mash together.

You can also use fantasy to explore deeper themes. For example, a story about grief might have ghosts or necromancy. A story about trust could have magical bonds that only work when someone is truly open. A story about identity might involve shapeshifters or glamour spells. In Romantasy, the fantasy is there to *reveal* the characters, not just entertain.

Let's talk creatures. This is where things get really fun. You're not stuck with dragons and unicorns—unless you want to be. You can invent your own magical species, or remix familiar ones in new ways. A phoenix who's reincarnated with memories of a lost love. A mermaid whose song binds people to her will. A forest spirit that wears the face of someone you once loved. Creatures can be enemies, allies, metaphors, or even romantic leads themselves.

Want to generate a bunch of fantasy creature ideas in seconds? Ask ChatGPT something like, "Invent ten original magical creatures for a Romantasy world that's full of sorrow and beauty." Watch what shows up. Maybe you'll get dusk-beasts that appear only at twilight and feed on regret. Or whisper-moths that nest in the mouths of liars. Suddenly you've got something weird, wild, and emotionally evocative. And that's exactly what readers want from this genre—something *new* that still makes them *feel.*

The same goes for lore. Your world doesn't need a detailed three-thousand-year timeline. But it should feel *old*. Lived in. Steeped in stories. Readers love the sense that this place existed before the lovers met—and will go on after, changed because of them. Give your world myths, legends, sacred texts, ghost stories, or old prophecies. These don't just add flavor—they add *layers*. Maybe your heroine grew up hearing a bedtime story that turns out to be a real legend tied to her bloodline. Maybe there's a star that appears in the sky whenever soulmates are near. Maybe there's a god who once loved a mortal and now punishes all who try to do the same.

You don't need to explain every detail. In fact, the best Romantasy worlds are built with a bit of mystery. Show glimpses. Hints. Half-remembered songs and broken statues. Use your fantasy world like poetry—let it hint at things too big to name. Your readers will fill in the rest with their own dreams.

Another great trick is to tie geography to emotion. Think about the places your characters will travel through. A desert that drains magic. A forest that listens. A city built on the bones of an ancient betrayal. Don't just make locations cool—make them *resonate*. Give each major setting a vibe, a history, a secret. Make them more than places. Make them characters.

And remember: everything you build should be *in service of the story*. You don't need to invent a magic system just because you feel like you have to. Invent it because it reveals something about the characters. If your lovers are both afraid of losing control, maybe magic in your world *requires* surrender. If one character doesn't believe in love, maybe magic can't even *see* them—until they change.

When you're trying to write a Romantasy in a single day, don't get overwhelmed by trying to build an encyclopaedia. You don't need *everything.* You need *just enough* to create a world that feels rich and real to you. Focus on what matters to the romance. Build the fantasy that reflects the heart of your story.

And anytime you feel stuck, you know what to do. Fire up ChatGPT and say, "Help me design a world where love is dangerous and magic is dying." Or "Describe three magical regions and how they influence the people who live there." Use the results to build momentum, not limits.

Fantasy isn't about creating rules for their own sake. It's about building a world where emotional truths get to wear beautiful masks and ride winged beasts through cursed skies. It's about making feelings *big enough to be seen*. And that's exactly what makes Romantasy such a joy to write.

In the next chapter, we'll dive into how to structure all this magic and emotion into a story that flows. Because now that you have a love story and a fantasy world, it's time to start shaping the journey.

Let's talk structure.

Structuring Your Romantasy for Maximum Impact

Structure isn't the enemy of creativity—it's the rhythm that lets your story dance. Especially when you're writing a Romantasy, where emotions run wild and magic bends the rules of reality, structure becomes the thing that keeps your story from floating off into chaos. It gives your characters space to grow, your romance time to breathe, and your plot the momentum it needs to sweep readers off their feet.

Let's be honest, Romantasy is a genre that *wants* to go big. Epic battles, slow-burn chemistry, curses that last centuries, kisses that change fate—you're dealing with a lot. And when you're writing it in a day, you don't have time to meander. You need a structure that supports all the emotional highs and fantastical twists while still moving like a river. It needs to flow forward. Always.

So how do you structure a Romantasy in a way that makes readers fall in love *and* hang onto every page like it's a magical rope bridge over a sea of dragon fire?

You start by thinking of two journeys unfolding at the same time: the *romantic* arc and the *fantasy* arc. They're like two vines twisting around each other, feeding into each other, tightening tension together. When one of them surges forward, the other should react. That's how you get that satisfying feeling where every chapter gives you both plot and heart.

One of the simplest ways to structure this is using the classic three-act format—because, surprise, it works beautifully for Romantasy. But here's the trick: you're not just structuring *a plot.* You're structuring an *emotional experience.*

Act One is where you set the stage. This is where we meet your main character and see the world through their eyes. It's where we understand what's missing, what they long for, and what their fears are. It's also where they meet—or reencounter—the romantic lead. Whether they clash instantly or feel the pull of destiny from the start, this is where the tension begins. Meanwhile, the fantasy stakes start to shimmer in the background—an oncoming war, a dangerous curse, a prophecy, a relic, a rebellion. Something stirs. Something calls them to act. The act ends with a decision: they cross the threshold. They step into the unknown. The journey begins.

Act Two is where everything tightens. The romance grows—or frays. The world expands. The magic complicates things. Your characters face trials, temptations, enemies, and each other. This is your slow burn zone. Your "almost kiss" moment. Your "I hate you but I can't stop thinking about you" scene. But it's also where the stakes rise in the fantasy world. They uncover secrets. They fail. They're tested. The midpoint—the heart of the story—is often a moment of emotional intimacy or catastrophic separation. Sometimes both. This act ends with a low point. A betrayal. A loss. A truth revealed. The lovers are torn apart, literally or emotionally. Something breaks.

Act Three is all about choices. Your characters now know what they want—and what it will cost. This is where they must earn each other. The world demands sacrifice. The prophecy comes due. The curse tightens. The villain strikes. And in the middle of all that chaos, your characters have to find their way back to each other—or decide to let go. It's the climax of both the fantasy arc *and* the romance. The final confrontation, the ultimate act of love, the moment where everything changes. Then you land the story. Maybe they win the war and ride off together. Maybe they part ways, changed forever. Maybe they die for each other and live on in legend. Whatever it is, the ending has to feel *true.*

When you're writing fast, structure is your secret weapon. You don't need to plan every scene ahead of time, but you do want to know your anchor points—what kicks things off, what breaks their hearts, and how it all ends. Those become your tentpoles. You can fill in everything else as you write, using ChatGPT to help flesh out scenes or transitions as needed.

For example, once you've got your beats, you can ask ChatGPT to help you write toward each one:

"Write a scene where the hero realizes he's falling for the enemy princess."

"Write the moment they discover the magical artifact is tied to their love."

"Describe the confrontation with the villain where one lover sacrifices something huge for the other."

It's like story scaffolding. You're not improvising wildly—you're *building*, with intention.

And don't forget pacing. Romantasy doesn't need to rush, but it also can't drag. Keep your story moving forward with new reveals, shifts in relationship dynamics, or changes in magical stakes. If a scene doesn't push the romance *or* the fantasy arc forward, cut it. Or make it do more.

A good rule of thumb? Every chapter should:

- Deepen the emotional stakes between your leads
- Reveal something new about the world or the problem they face
- Change something—emotionally, magically, or both

Even if the change is subtle, readers should *feel* the story turning beneath their feet.

Let's also talk about *echoes*—those little patterns that repeat through a story to give it cohesion. Maybe a phrase one character says in Act One comes back in the final scene, loaded with new meaning. Maybe the magical element that first brought them together is also what threatens to tear them apart. These echoes make your story feel *designed,* even if you wrote it in a whirlwind.

And when you're working with ChatGPT, you can actually use it to help find those echoes. Ask it, "What are emotional motifs I can use throughout this story?" or "How can I mirror the first meeting between my characters in the final scene?" ChatGPT is great at spotting narrative symmetry and offering ways to make your story feel more emotionally satisfying.

One of the best parts about Romantasy is that its structure is allowed to be big, dramatic, and mythic—but still deeply intimate. You can have world-ending stakes *and* a whispered apology. A battle of armies *and* a single tear. That's what readers come for. That's what makes the genre feel both sweeping and personal.

So don't be afraid to go big with your structure. Plan a fall, a rise, a twist, a test. Build the kind of story that makes a reader stay up all night because they *have* to know what happens next. And let the romance and fantasy move in rhythm—sometimes in harmony, sometimes in conflict, but always *together.*

In the next chapter, we'll explore how to write the hero's journey—with romance at the core. Because your protagonist isn't just going on a quest. They're learning how to love in a world built to make it nearly impossible.

Let's take them on that journey.

Writing the Hero's Journey with a Heartbeat

The hero's journey has been around forever. You know the beats—call to adventure, trials, temptation, transformation, return. It's the classic arc where a character is pushed out of their comfort zone, tested, changed, and returns home (or to a new home) wiser, braver, stronger. But when you're writing *Romantasy*, the hero's journey isn't just about slaying monsters or discovering hidden powers. It's about opening the heart. It's about learning to love—not just someone else, but maybe even yourself.

In Romantasy, your hero's journey needs a heartbeat.

This is the genre where emotional vulnerability *is* strength. Your main character might start as a powerful mage, a street thief, a cursed royal, or a battle-hardened outcast—but whatever their role, what they *don't* have yet is connection. They don't know how to trust, or how to risk intimacy, or how to choose love over fear. That becomes the true journey. Yes, they'll face magical tests, dark forests, ancient prophecies—but the real transformation happens inside them, scene by scene, as they move from guarded to open, from alone to together.

Let's start by anchoring your hero. In the beginning of your story, they need to *want* something and *fear* something. These don't have to be the same thing, but they should create tension. Maybe they want revenge but fear losing control. Maybe they want peace but fear being vulnerable. Maybe they want to protect their people but fear their own power. This emotional blueprint will shape how they respond to love when it comes knocking.

Now layer in the call to adventure. Something has to push them out of their normal life—whether that's a literal invasion, a magical inheritance, or a fateful meeting with the romantic lead. Whatever it is, it forces your hero into motion. And here's where you start weaving in the heartbeat. If your main character meets their love interest early on, that character can become a symbol of the unknown. A test. A mirror. A reason to resist or surrender. They don't have to be a sidekick on the journey. They *are* the journey.

One of the key aspects of the hero's journey is *refusal of the call*—that initial hesitation. In Romantasy, this can show up as resistance to falling in love. Maybe they think it's a distraction. Maybe they've been burned before. Maybe love is dangerous in their world. But you want to plant the seeds early that love is going to be the thing that undoes them—and saves them. It's the path they'll deny, then slowly begin to crave.

As the story progresses, your hero will face *tests and allies*. Some of these will be fantasy-based—riddles, monsters, betrayals. But some will be emotional. Can they open up to the romantic lead? Can they trust someone with their truth? Can they choose softness in a world that rewards strength? These are your emotional checkpoints. And every time the hero fails or grows, the love story changes too.

Now, the midpoint. This is often where your hero gets a glimpse of what they could have—if only they were brave enough. Maybe there's a kiss. A confession. A quiet moment in the chaos. It's beautiful, but it's not safe yet. Because the real test is still coming. Right after that midpoint, you often hit the *fall*. Something goes wrong. A secret comes out. A betrayal cuts deep. Maybe the lovers are separated, or one of them pulls away. This is the dark night of the soul, not just for the world, but for the heart.

And here's where your hero transforms.

The classic hero's journey has a moment of death and rebirth—usually not literal, but emotional. Something inside your hero breaks, burns, collapses. This is the moment they realize what they've been doing wrong. Maybe they've been trying to control everything. Maybe they've been pushing love away. Maybe they've been protecting themselves from pain so hard that they've missed the only thing worth feeling. And now, they choose differently.

In Romantasy, that choice is *love.* They choose to fight for it. Risk for it. Say it. Prove it. The external climax—facing the villain, breaking the curse, saving the realm—usually overlaps with this emotional climax. The two arcs collide. The hero must act not just with power, but with heart. They can't win unless they've changed.

And then we reach the final return. In myth, the hero returns home with the elixir—a gift, a truth, a power. In Romantasy, they return with love. Or maybe they don't return at all—maybe they build a new home, a new world, with the person they've chosen. Maybe they sacrifice everything for one moment of truth. Maybe they get their happy ending—or maybe they don't, but their love still changed everything.

The point is: this journey isn't just external. It's emotional. Magical trials and romantic growth should be in constant conversation. If your hero learns something from a battle, let it affect how they speak to the love interest in the next scene. If their lover calls them out on something painful, let that fuel their next confrontation with a magical challenge. The world tests them. The love teaches them.

Let's pause here and say this: the hero's journey doesn't have to be about a traditional "hero." Your main character can be messy, reluctant, impulsive, deeply flawed. They don't need to save the world. They just need to be *changed* by the journey. And if love is part of that transformation—if it's the spark that forces them to confront who they really are—then you're writing a Romantasy that hits where it counts.

Now, if you're building this quickly—trying to write the whole thing in a day—ChatGPT can be a huge help. You can ask it to map out the hero's journey with your specific concept in mind. Say, "Create a hero's journey outline for a Romantasy about a cursed prince who's afraid to love." You'll get a beat-by-beat guide. Then you can plug in your own character voice and plot details as you write.

Better yet, ask ChatGPT for emotional transitions. Try something like, "Describe a scene where the heroine realizes her need for control is destroying her only chance at love." Or "Write a turning point where the hero sees his power differently after a romantic betrayal." You'll get emotionally charged moments you can use to propel your character forward in both arcs at once.

If you want readers to remember your story, make them feel like they went on a journey *inside* someone's heart. That's what the best Romantasy does. It casts a spell with story, then breaks it with truth. It gives you the grandeur of fantasy with the intimacy of romance. The swords and the softness. The peril and the passion.

So as you write your hero, don't just ask what they're fighting. Ask what they're learning. What they're shedding. What they're risking. Ask who they are before love—and who they are after. That's the journey that matters.

In the next chapter, we'll bring your world to life, one enchanted stone and sky-drenched city at a time. Because love needs a place to burn, and fantasy needs somewhere to bloom.

Let's build your setting.

Creating a Magical World That Breathes with Life and Love

You don't need to create an entire continent or write a detailed historical timeline to make a magical world come alive. What you need is a world that *feels* lived in—a place that hums with mystery, beauty, danger, and, most importantly, emotion. In Romantasy, your world isn't just a backdrop. It's an extension of the love story. It reflects the emotional weather of your characters and reacts to their desires, choices, and fates. It doesn't just hold the romance—it shapes it.

So let's make your world breathe.

When we talk about worldbuilding in fantasy, it's easy to think in terms of scale. Kingdoms. Maps. Inventions. Systems of government. But when you're building for Romantasy, *atmosphere* matters more than exhaustiveness. Readers don't need to know every economic law or the name of every royal ancestor. They need to *feel* what it's like to walk through the forest where your characters fall in love. They need to hear the wind through the haunted ruins. They need to smell the roses that only bloom under moonlight in the garden where your lovers first touch.

This is worldbuilding with mood and meaning.

Start with one magical truth about your world. Just one. Something central. Something emotional. Maybe love is a magical force—rare and powerful. Maybe magic itself is dying, and only love can restore it. Maybe lovers are marked by glowing sigils when they touch. Or maybe the world is fractured, and magic is forbidden because of an ancient love story gone wrong.

That one truth is the seed. Everything else grows from it.

From there, think small before you think big. What does your main character's room look like? What kind of market do they walk through in the morning? Is there a song everyone knows, passed down from some magical myth? These little details are what make the world feel real. You don't have to describe every corner—just enough to let the reader dream.

And tie everything back to *emotion*. If your character is lonely, show it in the world. Maybe the city is cold, full of shadows and closed windows. If your character is in love for the first time, let the world brighten—magic blooms, stars appear in daylight, old statues seem to smile. Fantasy gives you permission to make the *setting itself* respond to feeling. Use that power.

Let's talk landscapes. Where do the romantic moments happen? The secret kisses, the silent goodbyes, the final reunions? Don't just drop them in convenient places—design places that *invite* emotion. A hidden glade that hums with old spells. A high tower that catches the morning light just so. A bridge that disappears at dusk, unless you cross it holding someone's hand. Make the world part of the poetry.

And don't forget history and myth. You don't need a full lore bible, but your world should have echoes of stories past. Legends, rituals, old prophecies. Maybe your characters fall in love under the same moon that once watched over a tragic royal affair. Maybe they re-enact a ritual not knowing what it means—until it binds them forever. These narrative layers give depth and richness. They make the world feel old, full of secrets, and so much bigger than just what's on the page.

This is also where you can lean on ChatGPT to do some of the heavy lifting. You can prompt it to generate specific world elements that match your story's tone. Try, "Give me ideas for a fantasy city built on floating islands where falling in love changes the weather," or "Describe a desert kingdom where magic is harvested through touch." ChatGPT will give you a variety of sensory-rich options. Pick what feels right. Mix and match. Reimagine it your way.

And let's talk about *rules*. Even in a dreamlike world, magic needs logic. Maybe not a hard system with rules and laws, but at least a *sense* of consequence. Magic should cost something, change something, or challenge something. If love is magical, what does it *do*? Does it bind souls? Unlock hidden memories? Attract monsters? Your reader will accept almost anything—*if* you stay consistent and grounded in the emotional truth of it.

Want a shortcut? Link magic to feelings. When the lovers fight, the magic falters. When they kiss, something unlocks. When one of them betrays the other, the world cracks open. When one lets go, the spell fades. This kind of emotional-magic feedback loop keeps your story intimate and fantastical at the same time.

Also consider what kinds of creatures, spirits, or relics live in this world—and how they fit into the love story. Maybe there are guardians who test couples, or enchanted mirrors that show a person's truest desire. Maybe there's a river that remembers every love story that ever happened on its shores. Maybe falling in love grants you the ability to hear someone else's thoughts—or feel their past pain.

What about obstacles? Worldbuilding should challenge your characters. If your lovers come from opposing magical orders, that tension should be baked into the fabric of your world. If love is cursed, let the geography reflect that—dark places, forgotten cities, haunted forests. If the magic is misunderstood, make the culture wary of emotion. Let the rules and locations of your world test the romance at every step.

Think of the world like a stage, yes—but also like a spell. A good Romantasy world *enchants* the reader. It draws them in not with complexity, but with intimacy and awe. It makes them feel like they've been somewhere beautiful and aching. Somewhere they want to go back to—even if it broke them a little.

You don't have to overbuild. Just build with care.

And don't forget, setting can *change* through the story. As your characters grow, your world can transform. A place that was once cold and forbidding might become warm and magical as love blooms. A kingdom once full of fear might start to hope again. Or maybe the world stays the same—but your characters see it differently, now that they're no longer alone.

That's how you make a world breathe.

A magical world in Romantasy isn't just where the story happens. It *is* the story. It reflects every tear, every touch, every moment of wonder. Build it like you're falling in love with it. Let your characters fall in love *within* it. And your reader will fall in love, too.

Developing Your Protagonist: The Lover, the Fighter, the Dreamer

A Romantasy protagonist is more than a hero. They're more than a chosen one, or a reluctant warrior, or a runaway royal with a secret. At the core of this genre, your main character is the lover, the fighter, and the dreamer all in one. They are someone on the edge of something extraordinary—torn between power and tenderness, survival and surrender, fear and longing. That's why readers fall for them. That's why they root for them. That's why they follow them through impossible worlds and aching choices. Because beneath the magic and the monsters, this is someone who *feels*.

So when you sit down to shape your protagonist, don't think first about what they *do*. Think about who they are when no one's watching.

Maybe they're the best swordswoman in the kingdom. But what if she can't bear to be touched because of a curse no one knows about? Maybe he's a gifted mage—but terrified of his own power because it once destroyed someone he loved. Maybe they're a runaway from a noble family, hiding their identity, yearning for a simple life, and yet pulled toward a destiny they never asked for. You're looking for contradiction. For vulnerability. For tension between who they pretend to be and who they really are.

A Romantasy protagonist often wears armor. Sometimes literal. Sometimes emotional. But the story you're writing is about *taking it off.* Piece by piece. Scene by scene. That's the heartbeat of this genre—not just external transformation, but deep, personal emotional change. The kind that hurts. The kind that heals.

Let's break down the three roles they play: the lover, the fighter, the dreamer.

The Lover is not always romantic at first. It's the part of your protagonist that *wants* to connect, even if they're scared to. This is where their empathy lives, even if it's buried under sarcasm or rage. This is the version of them that craves intimacy, trust, comfort. It's the part that softens when someone sees past their walls. This part of your character doesn't have to be obvious. It might show up in how they care for a wounded animal. Or the way they remember the smell of someone's hair after they're gone. Or how much it wrecks them to be touched kindly. The Lover is the part of them that can—and eventually will—fall.

The Fighter is the survivor. The part that keeps the rest of them standing. This is where your character's strength comes from, and it's shaped by pain. Maybe they had to fight to be heard. Maybe they were raised in a brutal system. Maybe they've been hunted, exiled, cursed. Whatever shaped their fight, it's what makes them brave. But it also isolates them. The Fighter resists softness. The Fighter doesn't ask for help. That's the tension in Romantasy—when the Fighter falls in love, they have to choose to be vulnerable without losing their edge. They have to learn that love doesn't make them weak. It makes them *human.*

The Dreamer is the part that still believes in more. In hope. In beauty. In freedom. This is often the quietest part of the protagonist—especially if the world has crushed them. But it's there. The part of them that wonders what it might be like to not run. To not fight. To be held. To be seen. To belong. This is the part of your character that magic wakes up. The part that love revives. When this part comes forward—usually around the midpoint of your story—it cracks everything open.

Your job, as the writer, is to let these three aspects collide. Sometimes the Fighter will win. Sometimes the Lover will. Sometimes the Dreamer will take a risk that terrifies the Fighter. Sometimes the Lover will beg the Dreamer to stop hoping. And then, in the climax, all three come together. That's when you get the hero's fullest form—the whole person. Changed. Whole. Awake.

When building this character, ChatGPT can be your partner in deepening their psychology. Try a prompt like, "Help me build a Romantasy protagonist who is emotionally guarded but secretly craves connection," or "Give me emotional flaws for a protagonist who was raised to be a weapon but wants to be loved." Ask for backstory ideas. Ask for formative moments. Ask for internal contradictions. You'll get suggestions that help you move from a trope to a full, beating heart.

And once you've got your protagonist's emotional core, give them a *want* and a *need*. This is classic storytelling, but it's especially potent in Romantasy. What they *want* might be power, revenge, safety, escape. What they *need* is usually love, forgiveness, trust, truth. The story is about their journey from want to need—learning that what they thought would save them isn't what they actually needed. The magic helps reveal that. The romance demands it.

Also, consider how your protagonist's internal struggle is reflected externally. A character who doesn't trust anyone might live in a tower surrounded by wards. A character who fears loss might refuse to use magic because it's tied to grief. A character who believes they're unlovable might be under a literal curse that keeps people from remembering them. Romantasy lets you turn emotional truths into plot elements, into worldbuilding, into tension.

Now let's not forget voice. Your protagonist's point of view needs to *feel* alive. Whether you're writing first-person or third, the voice should carry their wounds, their wit, their longing. Don't make them perfect. Let them be bitter. Let them be wrong. Let them fail. But let us *feel* with them. Show us what they notice. What they remember. What they can't say out loud. In Romantasy, the reader falls in love with the protagonist too—not because they're flawless, but because they *ache*.

You might be tempted to build a big, flashy lead. The most powerful mage. The deadliest assassin. The heir to a broken kingdom. And that's all fine—*if* you give them something human underneath. A fear. A desire. A regret. Without that, no amount of cool powers or epic destiny will make readers care.

And finally, design your protagonist to *grow*. Not just to defeat a villain or master magic, but to open up. To let love in. To become more whole. The journey they go on should strip away the lie they've been living. And the person who helps them see that? The romantic lead. Not by fixing them. Not by saving them. But by challenging them to be more than their past.

The best Romantasy protagonists are unforgettable because they feel real—even when they're doing impossible things. They're vulnerable and brave. They long and they resist. They kiss with fire and bleed with hope. They are the reason we read these stories.

Creating the Romantic Lead: The One They'll Risk Everything For

Every great Romantasy has that one character who steals your breath the second they walk onto the page. Not just because they're beautiful or brooding or wrapped in mystery, but because something about them *aches*. They carry a presence, a pain, a promise. You *know* your protagonist's heart is in danger the moment they meet. And so is yours.

That's the romantic lead—the one they'll risk everything for.

In Romantasy, this character isn't just a love interest. They are a force of change. A mirror. A spark. Sometimes a test. Sometimes a salvation. And if you build them right, they'll linger in your reader's mind long after the story ends.

So how do you create someone who feels like a romantic destiny and a character in their own right?

Start by refusing to make them perfect. The romantic lead should have their own flaws, their own wounds, their own desires that have nothing to do with the protagonist. They didn't come into existence just to be loved. They have history. Secrets. Regrets. And they don't always do the right thing. In fact, they *shouldn't.* A romantic lead who's always good, always gentle, always right? Boring. You want the person who surprises the protagonist, who challenges them, who pushes back and makes them think.

A good romantic lead also has something *hidden*. Something the protagonist can't see at first—or refuses to. Maybe it's a past they won't speak of. Maybe it's the truth about their identity, their family, their curse. Maybe it's just the depth of their feelings, locked behind a guarded expression. That hidden part creates tension. Readers keep reading because they want to know what's under the surface—and what will happen when it finally breaks free.

Another thing to consider: the romantic lead should have agency. That means they make choices. Big ones. Hard ones. They're not just tagging along, reacting to the protagonist. They have goals. Maybe those goals conflict. Maybe they start on opposite sides. But the romantic lead's actions should shift the plot in real ways. Maybe they steal something vital. Maybe they betray someone to protect the protagonist. Maybe they disappear just when they're needed most—and return changed.

They should also grow. Not just fall in love. Love is part of their journey, but it shouldn't be their only arc. Maybe they need to let go of guilt. Maybe they need to believe they're worthy. Maybe they need to fight for something other than vengeance. The story should transform them, too. So that by the end, they're not just in love—they're *different* because of it.

Now, chemistry. This is where things get electric. The best romantic leads create instant friction with the protagonist—not necessarily sexual (though it can be), but emotional. They make the protagonist react in ways no one else does. They unsettle them. Amuse them. Infuriate them. They *see* them in a way no one else has. And when they touch? Whether it's a graze of fingers or a first kiss or a battlefield confession—it *matters*. Because it's not just about physical attraction. It's about *recognition*.

Try giving your romantic lead a strength that makes the protagonist uncomfortable. Maybe they're too honest. Or too unpredictable. Or too unshakably calm in chaos. And give them a vulnerability that sneaks through. The thing they try to hide. The thing that slips out when they're tired, scared, or too in love to pretend anymore.

Need help fleshing that out? Ask ChatGPT to brainstorm. Try: "Give me character traits for a Romantasy love interest who is powerful but emotionally distant," or "Create a romantic lead who hides a dangerous secret from the protagonist." You can even prompt: "Write a scene where the love interest lets down their guard for the first time." It'll give you tone, tension, and texture you can adapt into your own story voice.

Don't be afraid to choose a trope, either—enemies-to-lovers, forbidden love, the childhood friend, the royal guard, the fated mate. These are tools, not clichés. The key is to make the love interest *specific.* Give them layers, quirks, beliefs, flaws. What do they fear? What do they want? What would they never forgive—and what would they forgive in this one person?

And don't forget the *moments.* Readers remember the looks across a crowded room. The hand clasped too long. The line whispered in a quiet room. The moment one of them pulls the other behind a wall to hide from danger—but neither moves after the danger passes. Romance lives in the *small.* So build those moments in. Let the world pause around them, even if only for a breath.

Also, make sure your love interest has their *own* conflicts. Maybe they're supposed to marry someone else for political reasons. Maybe they're hiding a dangerous bloodline. Maybe loving the protagonist will destroy their magic. Whatever it is, it needs to hurt. Love in Romantasy should *cost* something. That's what makes it feel earned.

Now let's talk *choice.* At some point, the romantic lead should have the option to walk away. To choose safety. Power. Revenge. Silence. And they don't. They choose the protagonist. Not because they're perfect, but because they *see* them. And that choice is what makes the romance feel real.

So many Romantasy love stories fall flat because the love interest is too passive or too convenient. Don't do that. Make them unforgettable. Give them moments where they stand up. Break down. Burn bright. And make sure that, even when they're in love, they're *still themselves.* That's what keeps the fire alive.

In the best Romantasy stories, the love interest is never just a goal or an obstacle. They are a *journey.* The protagonist doesn't just fall in love with them—they discover who they are through them. And when the love interest *chooses* them back, with all their flaws and fears and mess? That's the real magic.

In the next chapter, we'll explore how to design side characters who matter—because no Romantasy story lives on just two hearts alone.

Let's build your supporting cast.

Inventing Compelling Side Characters with Secrets and Purpose

Your main characters are in the spotlight, sure—but every star burns brighter when surrounded by a vivid constellation. In Romantasy, your side characters are more than set dressing or comic relief. They're the ones who make your world feel real. They're the ones who test, challenge, support, and sometimes betray your protagonist. And when done right, they're the ones your readers get unexpectedly attached to. Sometimes even more than the leads.

Side characters are the heartbeat of your world. They carry its stories. They whisper its history. They pull your protagonist in deeper—and they each come with their own dreams, fears, and secrets. That's the key word here: **secrets.** Because in a world full of magic, destiny, and high emotional stakes, no one should be simple. Everyone should have something they're hiding.

Start by asking yourself: who surrounds your protagonist?

There's probably a best friend. Maybe a sibling. A mentor. A rival. A fellow soldier. A bitter servant. A mysterious traveler. A royal who doesn't want the crown. These are the people who shape your protagonist's worldview. Who hold the pieces of the past. Who represent the choices not taken. But they also need to matter in their own right.

So don't build them just to serve the plot. Build them to serve *themselves.*

Every side character should *want* something. Even if it's something small. Maybe the bodyguard wants to go home and see his family again. Maybe the scholarly advisor secretly wants the throne. Maybe the best friend is in love with the protagonist but too loyal to say it. Maybe the rival who mocks them at every turn is actually trying to protect them from something they know and can't reveal. Let them want things. Let them *need* things. Let their stories unfold behind the main one, like shadow plays that make your world feel dense and rich.

A great trick is to give every side character a piece of the world that only they reveal. Maybe one tells a myth that foreshadows the ending. Another shows us a different social class. Another unlocks a piece of magic the leads don't understand. Think of your cast like a map. Each one expands the reader's view just a little more.

And yes—give them secrets. Not just for the sake of drama (though it helps), but because that's how people work. A side character might act brave but be carrying a terrible guilt. Or they might seem loyal until they aren't. Or they might be the one who's known the truth all along, waiting for the right moment to speak. Secrets create tension. They make readers suspicious. They make betrayals believable. And when the truth finally comes out, it should matter.

You can use ChatGPT to brainstorm backstories for side characters easily. Ask, "Give me three side characters in a Romantasy world who each hide a painful truth," or "Create a cast of allies and rivals for my Romantasy heroine, each with their own agenda." The AI can give you scaffolding—then you go in and make them bleed. That's how you make them *real.*

Let's talk types for a moment—not stereotypes, but character functions that often appear in Romantasy:

The Loyal Confidant. The one who always has your protagonist's back... until they don't. Bonus points if they're in love with someone they can't have.

The Comic Relief. Not just for laughs, but to *ground* the story. The one who makes the sarcastic quips while everyone else is brooding. But even they should have layers—grief behind the smile, maybe, or a secret mission of their own.

The Mysterious Outsider. This is the character who knows more than they say. They hint at truths. They disappear and return changed. They challenge the leads in unexpected ways.

The Powerful Mentor. Often kind, sometimes ruthless. They might train the hero, or push them into danger to prepare them. And they usually carry a painful secret from their past.

The Villain's Second. Someone close to the antagonist—but not beyond redemption. This character can shift allegiances, provide insight, or die in a way that changes everything.

These are only starting points. Mix them. Flip them. Twist them. The best side characters feel like they have their *own* stories, running parallel to the main plot, even if we only see glimpses of it.

Now, how do they interact with the love story?

This is where things get interesting. Side characters can *complicate* the romance in powerful ways. Maybe they disapprove of the love interest. Maybe they see something the protagonist doesn't. Maybe they have a shared past with one of the leads. Maybe they're tied to a prophecy, a curse, a sacrifice. Don't let them sit quietly on the sidelines. Let them challenge, push, provoke, protect.

One of the best uses of a side character is to echo or contrast the main character's emotional arc. If your protagonist is terrified of love, maybe their best friend rushes into it. If your lead is learning to open up, maybe a side character is hardening. These mirrored journeys add depth and let readers experience more than one emotional angle.

And don't be afraid to *lose* them. Romantasy is often full of sacrifice. A side character's death can hit hard—if they mattered. If they had a voice. If they made readers laugh, or cry, or shout in frustration. Or maybe their betrayal is the wound that haunts the protagonist into Act Three. Or maybe they come through at the last moment, saving the world at the cost of everything they wanted. These moments don't just move the plot. They leave a mark.

Your story may only be focused on the main characters, but the more it *feels* like others are living full lives around them, the more immersive your world becomes. Don't write cardboard cut-outs. Write people. People who live, love, lie, hope, fight, and *fail*. Just like your protagonist. Just like us.

And when you get stuck, remember: every side character is someone's main character. They just happen to be walking through *this* story instead.

Tropes You'll Love: From Enemies-to-Lovers to Forbidden Romance

Romantasy and tropes go together like fire and moonlight. They're not clichés—they're storytelling spells. When done right, they spark recognition and craving. Readers don't roll their eyes when they see "enemies-to-lovers" or "the one bed" moment coming—they *lean in*, heart racing, hoping for the twist that will make it feel fresh, raw, earned, and unforgettable.

Tropes are the emotional shorthand of this genre. They carry weight because we know what they promise. But the best part? You get to play with them. Subvert them. Push them until they break, then build something better from the ruins. Let's dive into the tropes that rule Romantasy—not as limitations, but as ingredients. You choose which to mix. You choose how to season them with your characters, your world, and your voice.

Let's start with the big one: **Enemies-to-Lovers.** This is the crown jewel of Romantasy. There's nothing quite like two people who would rather kill each other than kiss—until they do both. The magic here is in the tension. Every glance becomes a threat, every touch an accident, every moment of softness a betrayal. Maybe they're from rival kingdoms. Maybe one is hunting the other. Maybe they were childhood friends turned enemies by fate. Whatever the setup, the payoff only works if their reasons for hating each other are real—and so are their reasons for falling. Make the stakes high, the insults clever, the betrayals sharp. But give us those cracks. Those stolen moments of vulnerability. Those tiny glimpses of affection that grow too dangerous to ignore. Let them fall like it's the last thing they ever wanted—and the only thing they ever needed.

Next up: **Forbidden Love.** This one hurts in all the right ways. Think lovers on opposite sides of a magical war. A healer who falls for the cursed prince. A mage who breaks every law to be with someone who doesn't even believe in magic. Forbidden love isn't just about being told "no"—it's about *knowing* the cost and still reaching out. The fear of discovery. The whispered promises in the dark. The ache of loving someone you're not allowed to touch. Make the danger real. Make the consequences terrifying. And when they choose each other anyway? Let it feel like rebellion and redemption rolled into one.

Then there's **Fated Mates.** A trope straight from fantasy's mythic roots. Two people destined by magic, stars, gods, or blood to be together. This can feel romantic and oppressive at once, and that's where the tension lives. What if one of them doesn't want the bond? What if being fated feels like a prison? Or what if they fall in love *before* they learn they're fated—and now everything feels too easy, too unreal? Play with the idea of fate. Break it. Fight it. Let love win not because it was destined, but because it was *chosen.*

The One Bed. Yes, it's a classic. Yes, it's been done. But it works for a reason. Two characters forced into uncomfortable proximity? The potential for tension, awkwardness, trust, and a thousand unspoken feelings? Perfection. Whether it's in a ruined temple, a forest cabin, or an enchanted cave, this scene gives you the chance to strip your characters down—emotionally, not just physically. Maybe they talk through the night. Maybe they don't speak at all. Maybe they wake up tangled in ways that surprise them both. It's not about the bed. It's about *what happens to their hearts while they lie there.*

Touch-Starved or Emotionally Guarded Love Interests. There's nothing quite like the slow unraveling of a character who's never been shown softness—until now. Maybe they flinch at first. Maybe they joke it off. Maybe they break down after the smallest gesture of kindness. This trope is delicious when paired with a more emotionally open protagonist. It's all about patience, tension, and the way love seeps in where armor used to be.

The Slow Burn. Oh, the agony. The delicious agony. This is for when you want to draw out every glance, every near-kiss, every almost-confession. Let the characters resist it. Deny it. Get close, pull away. Let them argue, protect, save, wound. Every interaction builds until the reader is *begging* for them to admit what they feel. The slow burn only works when the characters are constantly changing—growing, pushing each other, becoming more than they were. When they finally give in, it should feel like a dam breaking.

Love Triangles. Often controversial, but when done well? Devastating in the best way. The trick here is to make both options compelling—and different. One might be safe. One might be dangerous. One might represent the past, the other the future. One might challenge, while the other comforts. The triangle works best when it's not just about *who* the protagonist loves, but about *who they are* when they're with each person.

The Protective Moment. Whether it's a shield raised in battle, a magic spell thrown in panic, or a whispered threat to someone who dares to hurt the one they love—this trope hits hard. Readers *live* for the moment someone says, "Don't touch them," and means it. This isn't about dominance. It's about vulnerability, devotion, fear of loss. It's a reminder that in a world full of danger, this one person *matters*.

Amnesia, Curses, and Reincarnation. These are your high-concept tropes. Done right, they bring tragedy, fate, and longing into the mix. A lover who forgets. A curse that erases touch. A soulmate who dies and is reborn again and again. These tropes let you play with memory, destiny, and the idea that love transcends time and magic. Just make sure you ground the drama in emotional truth—otherwise it feels too big, too distant. Of course, you don't have to stick to one trope. Stack them. Subvert them. Let your story start as enemies-to-lovers and twist into forbidden love. Let your fated mates reject destiny and still choose each other anyway. Let the one-bed scene *fail* the first time, then destroy us when it finally lands later.

Tropes work best when you use them to dig into the emotional core of your story. Not just because they're fun (though they are), but because they reveal who your characters are. How they change. What they need. What they're terrified of. If you need help choosing or blending tropes, ask ChatGPT. Try, "What Romantasy tropes would work for a story about a cursed thief and a runaway royal?" Or "Give me ideas for how to subvert the fated mates trope in a tragic love story." Let the ideas pour in. Pick what resonates. Build from there.

Tropes are tools. Use them with love. Use them with purpose. And never be afraid to lean into the feelings they unlock—because Romantasy is all about big emotion wrapped in magic and myth.

Tropes You Can Twist: Making the Familiar Feel New Again

Tropes are like spells—you can cast them straight, or you can twist them into something unexpected. And in Romantasy, that twist can make the difference between a story that feels predictable and one that feels unforgettable. Readers love tropes because they offer comfort and emotional payoff, but they also love being surprised. They want the rug pulled out from under them—right after they've gotten cozy on it.

Twisting a trope doesn't mean mocking it or turning it on its head just for shock value. It means finding the *truth* underneath the familiar shape, and asking, "What if this went somewhere we haven't seen before?" It's about honoring what readers love while refusing to hand it to them on autopilot.

Let's start with one of the biggest: **Enemies-to-Lovers.** This trope works because it's rooted in tension and transformation. But the twist? Maybe they *don't* fall in love after they stop being enemies—maybe they fall in love *while* they still hate each other. Maybe they never stop being enemies at all, and that's the tragedy. Or what if the protagonist thinks they're enemies, but the love interest has never truly wanted to fight—just to protect something the protagonist doesn't understand yet? Flip the balance of knowledge, or make the "enemy" the one who sacrifices the most.

Fated Mates is ripe for subversion. The standard version promises cosmic certainty—but what if one of them *rejects* the bond? What if the magic gets it wrong, or is manipulated? Or what if they fall in love with someone else first, then discover their "true" mate? Suddenly, the choice between fate and free will becomes painful and charged. Or twist it further: what if fated mates are meant to destroy each other? Now you've got a story built on both longing and doom.

Then there's **The Chosen One.** We all know this one: the hidden heir, the one with secret power, the key to everything. But what if the chosen one doesn't want the role—*and sticks to that refusal*? Or they aren't the chosen one at all, and it's been a mistake from the beginning. Or maybe *both* lovers were told they were the chosen one—by different factions, with opposing prophecies. Now their love becomes a political and magical impossibility, rooted in lies neither of them told.

The Love Triangle doesn't have to be a game of elimination. What if it's not about who the protagonist loves *more*—but who challenges them to become their true self? What if the triangle isn't even romantic on all sides? Or what if the two rivals fall for each other, while the protagonist ends up alone—or with someone unexpected? Let the triangle evolve into something readers didn't see coming. Let it reveal character, not just chemistry.

Another favorite twist comes from **The One Bed Trope.** Instead of tension, what if it creates unexpected *comfort*? Maybe these two enemies share a bed and... nothing happens. No awkward glances. No closeness. Just silence. But that silence *changes everything.* Or maybe the one who's been pushing the other away finally falls asleep in their arms, and the one who's been patient this whole time quietly breaks. Because sometimes love isn't in what's said—it's in what isn't.

Secret Royalty is a classic fantasy move. But instead of the protagonist discovering they're royal, what if they learn they were *supposed* to be—then stolen away, and now must decide whether to reclaim something that no longer feels like theirs? Or they discover their love interest is royalty—but abdicated, disgraced, or cursed. Now the story isn't about ascending to power, but about deciding whether love is worth stepping into the past.

Let's talk about **Curses**. Most Romantasy curses are obstacles—someone is turned into a beast, or they'll die if they love, or they forget each other after sunrise. But what if the curse becomes *comforting*? What if being cursed makes someone finally feel *safe*, because it means no one can get close? Then love becomes terrifying in the opposite way—it threatens to break the walls they *wanted* around their heart. Or maybe love triggers the curse in the first place, forcing the characters to wonder whether their connection is worth the pain.

Protective Alpha Types. You've seen them. Powerful, stoic, borderline obsessive love interests who'd burn the world for the protagonist. You can keep the intensity, but flip the execution. What if your "alpha" is emotionally aware, gentle with boundaries, and lets the protagonist take the lead? What if the protection is subtle—political maneuvering, quiet guarding in the background—not growling declarations? Or maybe your fierce protector is the *softest* character, using magic to heal instead of fight. Power doesn't always have to look like dominance.

The Prophecy Trope practically begs for inversion. What if the prophecy is intentionally vague—or completely misunderstood? What if it's a riddle, and the lovers think it means they must *die* to save the world, but it actually means they must *live*—together? Or what if the prophecy is fake, designed to manipulate one of them into a role they were never meant to play? Give readers the prophecy—but then show them that destiny has a sense of humor.

And here's a small but powerful twist: **The Happy Ending.** You don't have to kill your characters off or deny them love to make it feel meaningful. But you *can* make that ending *earned.* Maybe they only end up together after surviving something no one believed they could. Maybe they don't get everything they wanted, but they find each other anyway. Or maybe their love *changes*—deepens, matures, becomes quieter and stronger after all the magic fades. Not every Romantasy needs a wedding. Some of the best ones end with a touch, a look, a promise.

Twisting tropes isn't about reinventing the wheel. It's about asking *why* a trope works, then digging under its surface. What emotional need does it fulfill? What assumptions does it rest on? And what happens if you take that expectation and *tilt* it just enough to make the reader gasp?

If you want help generating unique twists, you can feed your trope and theme into ChatGPT. Try, "Give me ten ways to subvert the forbidden love trope in a Romantasy where magic is illegal," or "What if my enemies-to-lovers story takes place in a world where truth is physically painful to speak?" Use the suggestions to kickstart your creativity, then follow your gut toward what feels emotionally rich and unexpected.

Because in the end, twisting tropes is about one thing: *surprising the heart.* Readers come to Romantasy because they want to feel. If you can take a story shape they think they know and make it hurt a little more—or heal a little deeper—you've done it right.

ChatGPT as Your Plot Architect: Outlining Scene by Scene

You've got your romance, your magic, your world. You've created characters who bleed and spark and collide. Now comes the part where many writers freeze up: *plotting*. That's where the fear kicks in. How do I go from this idea to an actual story? How do I figure out what happens, scene by scene, without losing the emotional thread? And how do I do it fast?

Here's the good news: you don't have to do it alone. ChatGPT can be your plot architect. A scene-by-scene companion who won't just throw tropes at you, but will help shape your Romantasy into something that breathes. You guide the vision—it helps lay the bricks.

Let's start with the big picture. You don't need every scene in place before you write. But having a loose map gives you confidence, especially when you're writing fast. Think of your plot as a spine, with the emotional arc and fantasy stakes braided together like nerve and bone. ChatGPT can help build this skeleton—and then flesh it out with scene prompts you can write toward.

Here's how to do it.

Start by telling ChatGPT what your story is *about*. Not just the premise, but the *feeling*. You might say:

"I'm writing a Romantasy about a royal mage and a cursed thief who are forced to journey together to break an ancient spell. It's enemies-to-lovers, with betrayal, longing, and a magical storm that threatens their world."

This gives the AI a strong emotional and narrative anchor. Now you can ask it:

"Can you outline this story in 20 scenes that balance the fantasy plot and the emotional romance?"

ChatGPT will give you a rough outline—probably beginning with a meet-cute or collision point, followed by escalating tension, shared trials, revelations, betrayal, heartbreak, and resolution. Not every suggestion will be gold. But some of them will surprise you. More importantly, it gives you something to react to. Something to shape, push against, and develop into your own.

You might get scenes like:

- Scene 1: The cursed thief attempts to steal a magical artifact and is caught by the royal mage.
- Scene 3: They're magically bound together and forced to travel to a hidden temple.
- Scene 6: A moment of accidental vulnerability during a dangerous storm.
- Scene 10: The mage discovers the truth about the thief's curse—and keeps it secret.
- Scene 14: A confrontation where truths are revealed, and they part ways.
- Scene 18: They reunite in the ruins of a city destroyed by the magical storm.
- Scene 20: They break the spell—not with power, but by choosing each other.

Now you have a spine. You can expand or adjust. And with each scene, you can ask ChatGPT for more detail:

"Write a summary of Scene 6. Make it emotionally tense and quietly romantic."

Or

"Give me three different emotional beats for a scene where they argue about whether magic can be trusted."

Use this to build *layers*. Your plot isn't just "what happens." It's what each moment *feels like*. The tension, the subtext, the silence between words. Let ChatGPT help you brainstorm that texture. It's great at coming up with twists, reversals, small emotional reveals. You're still the soul behind the story—it just gives you the blueprints.

Another approach? Start with the **emotional arc** and let the fantasy plot wrap around it. For example, list your character's key emotional shifts:

- They don't trust anyone.
- They start to feel something.
- They're betrayed.
- They choose to open up anyway.
- They fight for love.

Now ask ChatGPT to map fantasy events that would force those emotional beats to happen. You can say:

"Give me fantasy events that would cause these emotional shifts: 1. No trust → 2. tentative care → 3. heartbreak → 4. emotional risk → 5. love."

The result might be:

- 1: They're forced to work together under a binding spell.
- 2: One saves the other from a magical trap but doesn't explain why.
- 3: The mage finds out the thief has been hiding the key to breaking the curse.
- 4: The mage gives up their magical protection to save the thief.
- 5: They kiss under the collapsing stars, knowing they may not survive.

Now that's a plot that *feels*.

You can also break this down further by asking ChatGPT for **scene templates**. Think of them like writing exercises pointed directly at your story's heart. Try:

- "Give me a scene where the romantic lead accidentally reveals their vulnerability."
- "Describe a moment where the magic system creates conflict between the leads."
- "Write a high-stakes decision scene where both characters want the same thing but for different reasons."

It'll generate mini scenes or outlines you can either lift straight into your story or use as inspiration. You can even ask it to write dialogue, blocking, or subtext. Just don't let it take over the emotional voice. Let it *fuel* your voice.

And don't forget pacing. If things are moving too fast or too slow, ChatGPT can help restructure. You might say:

"Help me insert a bonding scene between two action-heavy chapters that deepens the romance without slowing the momentum."

Or

"What scenes could I cut or combine to keep the pace sharp while preserving key emotional moments?"

When plotting fast—especially for a one-day writing sprint—this kind of guidance saves time. It clears mental fog. You're not stuck staring at a blank page. You're having a conversation with a partner who throws out ideas until you find one that sticks.

One of the most helpful tricks? Ask ChatGPT to help you **mirror scenes**. This is where you echo a moment from earlier in the story—but the meaning has changed. Maybe they first touched hands to escape danger. Later, they touch the same way—but this time, it's a goodbye. You can say:

"Suggest a way to mirror the scene where they fall asleep reluctantly beside each other, but show how their relationship has changed by the end."

This kind of emotional architecture builds resonance. It makes readers *feel* the journey. And ChatGPT is surprisingly good at helping you find those echoes.

What if you don't even know where to start? Begin with a *single* idea—a moment, a feeling, an image. Then ask:

"What kind of story would grow around this scene: A thief caught stealing a magical ring that binds her soul to a mage sworn to celibacy?"

Boom. Now you're plotting.

Ultimately, ChatGPT can help you:

- Brainstorm your premise
- Develop your emotional arcs
- Design fantasy events that serve emotional growth
- Balance tension, pacing, and payoff
- Create outlines you can write into without freezing
- Suggest twists, callbacks, and mirrored scenes
- Keep going when you hit a wall

It doesn't replace your creativity. It *unlocks* it.

The Magical System: Building Rules without Rules Lawyering

Let's get one thing out of the way: your magic doesn't need to be a spreadsheet. You don't have to write a textbook on the arcane sciences to have a magical system that works. In Romantasy, the goal isn't to explain everything—it's to make it *feel* like it matters. Magic in this genre is emotional, symbolic, dangerous, and often beautifully messy. It exists to shape the world and deepen the love story—not to be dissected like circuitry.

So if you've been worrying that your magical system isn't "hard" or detailed enough, relax. In Romantasy, it's not about lawyering—it's about *meaning*.

Start by asking what magic *feels like* in your world. Is it forbidden? Sacred? Fading? Wild? Genetic? Does it hurt to use? Does it reveal truth or hide it? Does it come from love, blood, nature, gods, grief, or desire? Magic should be more than a tool—it should reflect your story's emotional core.

For example, if your protagonist is afraid of intimacy, what if magic requires emotional openness? If your lovers are torn apart by fate, what if magic lets them see each other's dreams, but only while they sleep? These connections create resonance. The magic doesn't have to be logical—it has to *matter.*

One of the most powerful moves in Romantasy is to tie magic to *emotion*. Magic that responds to feeling rather than formula. Maybe the more someone loves, the more powerful they become—but with that power comes consequences. Maybe magic leaks when someone lies. Maybe heartbreak makes the world crack. When emotion and enchantment are linked, every scene has more weight.

But okay, yes—there should be *some* rules. Even the most intuitive, dreamlike system needs boundaries. Why? Because rules create tension. If magic has no limits, then nothing has stakes. Love becomes too easy. Conflict melts away. So ask yourself: what can magic *not* do in your world? What happens when it's used too much, too selfishly, too soon? What are the costs?

Maybe magic shortens your life. Maybe it binds you to the one you cast it on. Maybe it opens your mind to voices you can't silence. Maybe healing someone transfers their pain into you. These rules don't have to be complicated. They just have to push your characters into hard decisions.

If you're stuck, ChatGPT can help generate boundaries that match your theme. Try:

"Give me five emotional limitations for a Romantasy magic system where love enhances power."

You might get:

- Magic grows unstable when used in fear
- Spells only last as long as trust does
- Forbidden love weakens your magic
- Magic leaves a mark on both caster and receiver
- The more powerful the spell, the more of your memory it costs

Now you've got rules that create conflict, story momentum, and emotional tension.

Another great use of magic in Romantasy is **symbolism**. Don't be afraid to let your system get poetic. Maybe when two people fall in love, their shadows blur. Maybe spells are cast by singing your deepest truths aloud. Maybe magic smells like a memory. These aren't rules—they're *textures*. They give your story flavor, tone, intimacy.

Think of magic like weather. It changes the mood. It complicates things. It can be sudden or slow, subtle or overwhelming. And just like weather, magic doesn't have to explain itself—it just has to make sense inside *your* world.

Still, consistency helps. If you introduce a rule, stick to it. If a character uses magic once and nearly dies, they shouldn't toss spells around like confetti two chapters later. Let the rules shape how your characters behave. Let them find clever ways around those limitations. That's where drama lives.

Another tip: make sure your protagonists aren't just using magic—they're *struggling* with it. Maybe they inherited it and fear they'll lose control. Maybe they *don't* have it and feel inadequate. Maybe the romantic lead has a kind of magic the protagonist has always been warned against. Let magic divide them. Let it bind them. Let it echo whatever emotional wound your story is working through.

You can also think of different **types** of magic. Maybe there's elemental magic and emotional magic. Light magic and shadow magic. Or perhaps it's based on ancient bloodlines. Maybe certain people can only do one kind of spell, and the love interest has something rare and dangerous that isolates them.

But don't overexplain. Drop hints. Let your world's understanding of magic feel as uncertain and mythic as real-world folklore. Maybe the rules are passed down in whispers. Maybe no one fully understands the cost. Maybe every spell cast leaves behind a question: "Was it worth it?"

And if you want to build something more detailed—maybe you love logic, systems, spell components, magical languages—go for it. Just make sure the complexity never drowns the feeling. Even the most rigorous magic system should serve the emotional arc.

When in doubt, ask ChatGPT to help test your ideas. Try:

"Does this magic system make emotional sense: where casting a spell transfers an emotion from one person to another?"

Or

"Create a system where magic is fueled by memories, and forgetting is the price of power."

These aren't just mechanics—they're story generators. They force choices. They create pain. And pain, in Romantasy, is the path to transformation.

Your magical system doesn't need to impress readers with its cleverness. It needs to *move* them. It needs to complicate the romance, deepen the characters, and make every kiss, fight, and decision feel *enchanted*.

So go ahead—write magic like a poet. Like a lover. Like someone who knows that rules are only interesting when they're hard to follow.

Romantic Conflict: Emotional Tension, Magical Obstacles, or Both?

Romance without conflict is a lullaby. Pretty, but forgettable. In Romantasy, where hearts meet magic, the conflict needs to pulse. It should ache, shimmer, provoke. This is a genre where love is tested by swords and secrets, where feelings flare as bright as firelight spells. To keep readers hooked, you don't just need romance—you need *romantic conflict.* Emotional tension. Magical interference. Maybe both, tangled so tightly the lovers can't tell where the hurt ends and the curse begins.

Let's start with emotional tension. This is the meat of any good romantic arc. It's not just about external problems keeping your characters apart. It's about *who they are* inside—what they fear, what they want, what they don't even know about themselves yet. You build tension when characters are drawn to each other *but.* That *but* is everything. It's the storm between their desire and their damage.

Maybe one of them doesn't believe they're lovable. Maybe the other has been betrayed too many times to trust easily. Maybe they've both been taught that love is weakness—and now every moment they grow closer feels like a kind of surrender. That's emotional conflict. They don't just fall in love. They *fight it.* And in every scene, that struggle plays out in glances, words not spoken, touches withheld.

You can layer in deeper emotional themes: shame, guilt, grief, fear of vulnerability, fear of being seen. The best romantic tension comes from characters who can't stop colliding—but aren't ready to be honest yet. They want too much. Or they want it too soon. Or they won't admit they want anything at all.

That's when the tension starts to burn.

Now let's talk magical obstacles. Fantasy lets you literalize emotion. A misunderstanding isn't just an awkward moment—it's a curse that erases memories of the relationship. A fear of connection isn't just emotional—it's a magical wall that physically repels intimacy. When you tie magic to romance, the conflict gets turned up. Because now it's not just about what they say or don't say—it's what they *can't* do. What the world won't let them have. What magic punishes them for trying to hold.

Maybe they're from rival magical factions. Maybe touching each other triggers an ancient prophecy. Maybe one of them is dying every time they kiss—but neither can stop. These aren't just fun ideas. They're ways to externalize emotional struggle. Fantasy lets you make the heartache visible, visceral. And Romantasy leans all the way in.

But here's the best part—you don't have to choose. The most powerful romantic conflict comes when emotional tension *and* magical interference feed off each other. Think about it. Maybe the magic isn't the enemy—it's just the mirror. The curse only activates when they lie to each other. The spell only breaks when they trust. The magical bond forces them to stay close—and they hate that they want it to last.

Let's say you've got two lovers who are emotionally guarded. One of them is carrying guilt, the other's afraid of abandonment. You throw them into a magical situation where they can read each other's thoughts. Boom. Now they can't hide. Every emotion they bury becomes impossible to ignore. The magic *forces* conflict—and, eventually, truth.

Or flip it. Maybe your characters fall in love slowly, tenderly—but the magic is racing ahead. A prophecy insists they must marry by the full moon or doom will fall. They're not ready. They *want* to be—but magic won't wait. Suddenly, their emotional timeline is out of sync with the magical one. That imbalance? That's tension.

Here's where ChatGPT can be useful again. You can prompt it like:

"Give me magical obstacles that echo a character's fear of intimacy."

"List emotional conflicts that could emerge between two magically bonded enemies forced to work together."

"What fantasy curses would force two people to confront their feelings before it's too late?"

You'll get ideas that push the story forward—and deeper.

Keep in mind: conflict should *evolve*. At first, the characters may argue because they don't trust each other. Then, because they do. Then, because they're terrified of losing what they've found. Love changes the shape of the tension. Let the conflict shift with the relationship. Maybe the first kiss feels like betrayal. Maybe the second kiss is all desperation. Maybe the third doesn't happen—because one of them walks away.

Each moment should feel like it *costs* something.

And don't forget internal conflict, either. Sometimes the biggest battle is inside a single character. Maybe they know the other person loves them, but they can't believe it. Maybe they sabotage every tender moment. Maybe they're afraid of what love will change. That tension is powerful when it plays out in stolen glances, unsent letters, spells that almost work, moments that almost happen.

These moments don't need to be big. Sometimes the softest scenes carry the sharpest edges. A healing spell that lingers too long. A whispered insult that hides a confession. A refusal to say "I love you" until the world is falling apart. Romantic conflict doesn't mean your characters are at war—it means they're unraveling, transforming, resisting what they want most.

And eventually, *something* has to break. The world. The curse. A heart. A belief. Something gives. That's what makes the payoff worth it. When they finally fall into each other's arms—when the magic lifts, or the truth is spoken, or the fear is overcome—it hits hard. Because we've *felt* every step.

One more thing: don't let the conflict be one-sided. Both characters should have a hand in the tension. They should both have blind spots. Both make mistakes. Both yearn. That shared responsibility makes the relationship feel balanced—even when it's messy.

So ask yourself, every time your characters get close:

What's keeping them apart right now?

Is it fear? Pride? A secret? A spell? A lie?

And what would it take to break that?

Then let the scene answer.

In the next chapter, we'll talk about how to write those scenes—the kisses, the arguments, the breaking points—with language that pulses, sings, and scorches.

Let's write some sparks.

Writing Kisses and Conflict: Balancing Tenderness and Tension

There's something electric about the moment before a kiss in a Romantasy story. It's where everything slows down and speeds up at once—where magic flickers at the edge of the page and the reader holds their breath. But here's the secret: a kiss isn't just about lips touching. It's about *what the kiss means.* What it costs. What it risks. And sometimes, what it breaks.

Writing powerful kisses in Romantasy is about capturing the pulse of both tenderness and tension. It's not about the mechanics. It's about the emotions crashing underneath—longing, fear, guilt, hope, desperation. You're not just describing a physical act. You're letting the reader feel the tremble behind it.

Let's start with the tension. Because in most great Romantasy stories, the kiss doesn't come easy. Maybe there's a magical boundary between the characters—something that makes touch dangerous. Maybe they're supposed to hate each other. Maybe one of them is holding back a truth that would change everything. These are the things that *fuel* a kiss scene. The kiss isn't just a release—it's a *reckoning.*

Ask yourself: What's unresolved between them when this kiss happens? What hasn't been said? What's being *avoided*? Then let the kiss force all of it to the surface.

You can build tension with pacing. Short sentences. Pauses. Near-touches. Interruptions. Dialogue that doesn't quite say what it means. Maybe one character leans in—but pulls back. Maybe the other touches their face but doesn't close the distance. That hesitation is powerful. It stretches the moment, lets readers lean in, lets their hearts pound. The kiss that *almost* happens can sometimes be more charged than the one that finally does.

And when it does? Make sure it's *earned.* That doesn't mean it has to be after a grand confession. It can happen in silence. In the aftermath of a battle. In the middle of a lie. But it has to feel like the characters couldn't *not* kiss in that moment. Like the pressure was too much. The distance too painful. The desire too real.

Let's talk tenderness now. The softness is what separates a Romantasy kiss from an action beat. It's in the details—how one character's hand shakes, how the other sighs against their mouth, how they breathe each other in like it's the first moment they've truly felt alive. Tenderness is in the vulnerability. In the slowness. In the way they let themselves be *seen.*

This is where you can write with rhythm. Use language that flows. Let the moment bloom on the page. Maybe the air tastes like snow. Maybe their heartbeats are louder than the storm around them. Maybe the magic between them calms, or flares, or glows. Let the kiss feel like the world has narrowed to just this—this touch, this gasp, this surrender.

But don't stop the story for a kiss. Let it *change* something. A kiss should never be static. It should either solve something—or complicate everything. Maybe it's the moment they realize they're doomed. Or the moment they stop lying. Or the moment they want something they can't have.

And don't forget conflict. Sometimes kisses *hurt.* Sometimes they happen in anger. In confusion. In betrayal. A kiss can be a promise—or a mistake. The best Romantasy kisses aren't always perfect. Sometimes they're messy. Sometimes someone pulls away first. Sometimes someone cries. That's what makes them unforgettable.

If you want help sharpening the tension, ChatGPT can absolutely help. Try prompts like:

"Write a Romantasy kiss scene where both characters want it but are afraid of the consequences."

"Give me a kiss scene interrupted by a magical flare neither expected."

"Describe a tender, slow kiss between two characters after a near-death moment."

ChatGPT will give you dialogue options, sensory details, variations on pacing. You can use that material to find your own tone. To refine what your characters are *really* feeling under the surface. Sometimes you'll use the words as-is. Other times, the scene it gives you is just the key that unlocks your own.

Let's look at how you can frame a kiss within a larger conflict. Maybe two characters finally admit their feelings—but just as they kiss, one of them realizes the other has been keeping a secret. Now the tenderness crashes into betrayal. Maybe a kiss happens under a curse—one that's supposed to strip away memories. Maybe they're kissing in the rain after surviving something impossible—but one of them knows it's the last time. These kinds of layered moments *hurt*, and that hurt is what makes Romantasy land so hard.

There's also space for joy. For relief. For surprise. A kiss can be sweet, giddy, even funny. Maybe it comes after days of awkwardness and tension, and when it finally happens, they both laugh. Maybe magic reacts, and the sky lights up. Maybe it's clumsy, human, full of nose bumps and apologetic smiles—and they love it anyway.

You don't have to write a kiss the same way every time. Maybe the first is hungry, angry, desperate. Maybe the second is slow, silent, reverent. Maybe the final kiss is soft because there are no more walls to tear down. Each kiss should feel like a *progression*—a physical expression of where the characters are emotionally. The goal isn't to be flowery. It's to be *honest*. What do the characters want in that moment? What are they afraid of? What do they know they'll regret? What are they willing to risk?

Let the kiss answer those questions.

Let it be the moment the reader knew was coming—but still didn't see *quite* like this.

Let it be the spell they didn't know they were waiting for.

And if you're stuck? Go back to the breath. The gaze. The hesitation. That's where the kiss begins. Not with lips—but with the heartbeat behind them.

Giving the Romance Real Stakes in a Fantasy World

Romance doesn't feel real without something to lose. In fantasy, that "something" can be just about anything—your soul, your freedom, your kingdom, your magic, your memories, your very identity. But what makes the romance in Romantasy really hit isn't how flashy the world is. It's how deeply the romance *hurts* when it's threatened. The dragons and spells might draw the reader in, but it's the love story—and what's at risk if it fails—that makes them stay up past midnight turning pages.

So how do you give the romance real stakes in a fantasy world? You make love dangerous. You make it powerful. You make it a choice that changes *everything*.

Let's start simple: what happens if the characters *don't* end up together? What's the cost—not just emotionally, but narratively? In Romantasy, love is often tied to fate, prophecy, curses, politics, or magical balance. So maybe the couple's union is the key to stabilizing magic across the realm. Maybe if they don't kiss under the moon before the eclipse, one of them dies. Maybe if they confess their love, an ancient pact is broken and war begins. These kinds of stakes raise the tension—but only if they *also* mean something personal.

Because at the core, it's not just about what happens to the *world*—it's what happens to *them*. Maybe the stakes are heartbreak. Isolation. Losing the last person who really saw them. Or maybe loving each other means becoming someone they fear: a queen, a monster, a weapon, a savior. The best romantic stakes twist the knife both ways—whether they choose love or walk away, *something* is lost.

And that's where fantasy gives you room to amplify. You can tie love to literal consequences. Magic that changes when emotions shift. Blood bonds that deepen with intimacy. Dreams that become real if shared. You can invent a rule that love awakens dangerous power—or suppresses it. That connection isn't just emotional—it's *structural*. It moves the world around them.

Let's say your lovers are from rival magical houses. If they're caught together, they'll both be disowned—or worse, enchanted into forgetting each other. Maybe the magic of their people is inherited through pure bloodlines, and loving each other means ending their family legacies. Or maybe one of them is cursed, and touching their soulmate causes them unbearable pain. These are high-stakes choices wrapped in emotion. And readers eat that up.

But don't stop at external threats. You can make the relationship itself the danger. What if being in love means unlocking a dark part of the protagonist? What if loving the wrong person is what triggers the end of the world? What if one character is fated to destroy the other, no matter how hard they try not to? These kinds of stakes are powerful because they're intimate. They force your characters to ask: *Is love worth the ruin it might bring?*

Now let's flip it. What if love is the *only* way to break the curse, heal the land, save the future? Suddenly, not falling in love becomes the problem. Now your characters are avoiding each other, not because they don't care—but because caring feels like surrender. That tension is golden.

Real stakes also mean real *change*. If the romance succeeds, what shifts? Does someone give up the throne? Sacrifice their immortality? Abandon their revenge? Even happy endings need a cost. Because in fantasy, power and love rarely come freely. And readers trust the payoff more when the journey felt like a fight.

This is where internal stakes come in—ones tied to identity, values, and fear. Maybe your protagonist has always believed that love makes you weak. That trust gets you killed. Falling in love, then, threatens their very sense of self. They must *change* to choose this person. Or maybe they've built their life on duty and control, and love threatens to undo all of it. Now the question becomes: *who are they willing to be* if it means being together?

You can also let the characters' goals be in conflict. Maybe the protagonist has to destroy an artifact to save the world—but the love interest is bound to that artifact. Maybe one character is sworn to protect a magical secret that the other was born to reveal. The romance can't exist in a vacuum. It should complicate the plot, and the plot should complicate the romance.

And here's the twist: the stakes don't always need to be deadly to feel real. Sometimes, all it takes is a *truth* that could end everything. A lie that's been festering. A sacrifice that wasn't supposed to mean anything—but now does. The stakes can be as small as a secret kiss that leads to betrayal—or as huge as a war ignited by love.

If you're struggling to raise the stakes in your story, try asking ChatGPT:

"What fantasy-based consequences might arise if two magical soulmates fall in love against a prophecy's warning?"

"Give me plot complications if a royal character falls for someone with outlawed magic."

"Suggest emotional stakes for a Romantasy couple where one is immortal and the other is fading away."

Let the answers spark new pathways. You don't need to use them all—just find the one that hits your heart and follow it.

And remember, stakes aren't just about risk—they're about *meaning*. The higher the emotional cost, the deeper the reader's investment. A Romantasy doesn't just ask, "Will they fall in love?" It asks, "Will they *survive* love?" And more importantly, "What will they become because of it?"

When the kiss comes, it should feel like a battlefield and a homecoming at once. When they say "I love you," it should be the most dangerous thing they've ever done.

So give your romance the kind of stakes that make readers ache. Because in the end, that ache is the real magic.

In the next chapter, we'll talk about how to use pacing to make that magic last—how to slow down, speed up, and shape your story so every emotional beat lands with impact.

Let's talk rhythm.

Pacing Your Romantasy: When to Pause, When to Burn

Pacing is the music your story dances to. In Romantasy, it's not just about how fast the plot moves—it's about *when* to linger, *when* to rush, *when* to hold a moment so tight it feels like time stops. The emotional core of your story depends on this rhythm. If you move too fast, the love feels shallow. If you move too slow, the tension dies. But when you get the pacing right? Every glance, every revelation, every kiss feels like fate.

Let's start with the fire: *the burn.*

Romantasy thrives on slow burn romance, on tension that builds and builds until it can't be ignored. You don't want your characters to fall into each other too quickly. Let them resist. Let them misunderstand each other. Let the world get in their way. Every obstacle adds fuel. Every almost-touch, every interrupted moment, every unsaid thing keeps the burn going. Readers love to ache with your characters. They want to feel the flutter, the frustration, the ache of anticipation.

But tension can't build forever without some kind of payoff. You need sparks. Releases of pressure. Small moments of closeness—followed by consequences. Maybe they kiss, then avoid each other. Maybe one opens up, then regrets it. These mini-bursts of intimacy keep the reader engaged without giving away too much too soon. Think of it like a heartbeat: build, release. Build, release.

Now flip it. Let's talk about *the pause.*

Pauses are where the heart of the story lives. After an intense scene—a battle, a betrayal, a confession—you need to breathe. These quieter moments are where characters reflect, process, change. Maybe it's a conversation by the fire. A memory shared. A scene of silence where one character watches the other sleep and realizes just how deeply they've fallen. These pauses deepen the emotional weight of the story. They give meaning to the chaos.

If you never pause, your story becomes exhausting. If you only pause, it drifts. It's about knowing when your characters need a moment—and when they're ready to be thrown back into the storm.

Fantasy gives you a lot of moving parts. Magic, quests, politics, danger. Romance can get lost if you don't pace it with care. One great trick is to tie your romantic progression to your fantasy plot beats. If the world is crumbling, let the characters get closer *because* of it. If they're forced on a journey together, use the lulls between battles for bonding. Let the magic literally or metaphorically reflect the pace of the relationship.

Here's an example of balance:

- **Scene 1**: An ambush. Tension. Distrust.
- **Scene 2**: They hide in a cave. One tends to the other's wounds. Paused intimacy.
- **Scene 3**: The next morning, they wake too close. Tension again. Distance reasserts.
- **Scene 4**: Magical trial. They must rely on each other. A look, a touch. Building.
- **Scene 5**: The kiss—but it's interrupted by a betrayal. Everything burns.

That rise and fall? That's pacing that breathes. That's pacing that *hurts*. In the best way.

You can use ChatGPT to help sketch this rhythm. Ask:

"Give me a scene sequence for a Romantasy story with rising romantic tension balanced with fantasy conflict."

"How can I space out key romantic moments so the story feels emotionally earned over 20 chapters?"

It'll help you structure without flattening the flow.

Another pacing tip: vary your *scene length and tone*. Long, sweeping emotional moments should be followed by something tight and urgent. A dreamy romantic pause might lead straight into a magical duel. That contrast keeps the story alive. Readers never get too comfortable—but they're always emotionally fed.

Pacing also depends on *character readiness*. Let them resist their feelings for a while. Let them give in too soon—and panic. Let them backtrack. Then let something force them to face what they really want. You don't need to space kisses or confessions by word count. You need to space them by *growth*.

When has the character earned this moment? When will it hurt the most? When will it heal the most?

Those are your pacing cues.

Don't forget your *world-building* moments. In fantasy, they're essential—but they can bog things down. So fold them into emotional beats. Don't just describe the city—they walk through it on the way to a tense meeting. Don't just explain the magic—have the romantic lead demonstrate it in a moment of protection or vulnerability. That keeps your pace from stalling.

Here's a quick metaphor: think of your Romantasy like a heartbeat. If it beats too fast, it becomes arrhythmic. If it beats too slow, it flat-lines. But when you pace it just right? It pulses with life. It draws readers in and keeps them there. Not by rushing to the next twist, but by letting each moment land.

Even action scenes can carry romantic pacing. Maybe they're fighting back-to-back. Maybe one saves the other. Maybe there's a pause mid-battle where they lock eyes and realize everything's changed. That's how you layer romantic tension into fantasy motion. That's pacing that multitasks.

And don't be afraid of *quiet climaxes*. Not everything has to end in fire and fury. Sometimes, the most powerful pacing move is to slow down completely. Let a character whisper a truth instead of shout it. Let the kiss happen in silence after everything else has fallen apart. That restraint? That pause? It can be devastating.

Want help structuring it? Try asking ChatGPT:

"Design a pacing structure for a Romantasy novel where the romance escalates through five major beats across a magical quest."

"What should the emotional highs and lows be if the romance is forbidden and slow-burning?"

Let the AI offer you scaffolding—then you shape the flow with your own instincts.

In the end, pacing is about *emotion*. Not just what happens—but when. Not just what they feel—but when they feel it. Let your story breathe. Let it sprint. Let it ache.

And most importantly, trust your reader. They'll wait for the kiss if the wait *hurts* in all the right ways. They'll savour the pause if it makes the next fire burn brighter.

Starting Your Story with a Hook That Feels Like a Spell

The first line of your Romantasy story isn't just an invitation. It's an enchantment. It should feel like the opening notes of a melody your reader didn't know they already loved. A little dangerous. A little beautiful. And impossible to stop listening to. When you're writing a story where love meets magic, your opening needs to shimmer. Not with glitter or over-explanation—but with *promise*.

So let's talk about crafting a hook that feels like a spell.

The biggest mistake writers make with opening lines is trying too hard to explain everything. The world, the magic system, the political conflict, the romance to come—it's tempting to try to front-load it all. But a great opening doesn't explain. It seduces.

Your first paragraph should make the reader feel something before they even fully know what's going on. A chill. A flutter. A flicker of danger. You don't need to dump the lore. You need to offer *tension*. A question. An image that lingers. A voice that won't let them go.

Let's break that down.

There are a few flavors of first-line magic that work especially well in Romantasy:

The Immediate Intrigue Hook

This is when you start with a mystery. Not a murder-mystery kind, but something that leaves the reader asking, "What's really going on here?" For example:

"The first time I kissed him, the stars flickered—and not in the poetic way."

Now we have romance. We have magic. And we have a *disturbance*. That last part? That's the key. It makes the reader lean in.

The Emotional Premonition Hook

These openings speak directly to the *feeling* your story promises. For Romantasy, that's often longing, danger, or a sense of destiny. Like:

"Everyone told me loving him would destroy me. They were right."

Now we're locked in. There's a relationship that already has stakes, already has pain, and the story hasn't even started yet.

The In-Motion Hook

This type throws us straight into a moment—often a physical one, or one full of sensory detail. Something is happening, and it's charged.

"She ran through the forest like the shadows knew her name."

You feel the motion, the atmosphere, the pulse. You don't know the rules, but you already *care*.

The Voice-Driven Hook

Sometimes it's not about what happens—it's about how it's said. The narrator's tone grabs you by the collar and refuses to let go.

"I should've let him die. But I was already too far gone to pretend I didn't love him."

Voice is chemistry on the page. If you get that right, readers will follow you anywhere.

Once you've got that first sentence, build your opening scene with the same enchantment. Keep things mysterious, emotional, and grounded in character. You don't need to spell out the entire magic system or the full backstory. Just give us one character, one strong feeling, and one thing that feels *off*. That's all you need.

Maybe your protagonist is about to steal something from someone they don't realize they'll fall in love with. Maybe they're attending a royal event, and the person they're sworn to hate is watching them from across the room. Maybe they're hiding a secret so powerful it pulses against their skin. Start there. Start where things *already hurt a little*. Where something's about to go wrong—or already has.

The most effective Romantasy hooks often include these elements:

- A *choice* about to be made
- A *lie* the protagonist is telling (to others or to themselves)
- A *sensation* that reveals magic (taste, sound, light, pain, vision)
- A *threat* to love, peace, identity, or power
- A *bond* that hasn't been acknowledged yet

You don't need all five. But even just *one* can draw the reader under your spell.

Now let's talk pacing within the first chapter. Don't rush to the inciting incident, but don't stall either. The reader should know by the end of Chapter One who they're following, what emotional wound they carry, and where the story tension lives. Not every detail—just the *tone*. Give them a reason to care. And don't forget the romantic thread. Even if the love interest doesn't appear yet, the *absence* of them can be felt. Maybe the protagonist mentions them in narration. Maybe there's a prophecy. Maybe they dream of someone they've never met. Set the stage for romance early—even if it's a shadow.

If you're stuck on your hook, ChatGPT is great for brainstorming. Try:

"Give me five Romantasy opening lines where the narrator is hiding something from the love interest."

"Write the first paragraph of a Romantasy where a kiss causes magic to erupt."

"Suggest an opening line for a Romantasy story with a dark prophecy and a forbidden love."

Let the AI give you options. Then follow the one that gives you a gut reaction.

And remember: a hook doesn't have to be *loud*. It just has to *echo*. It should leave a little residue behind. A tingle. A question. A sense that something important just started.

Because in Romantasy, we're not just starting a story. We're casting a spell.

Using ChatGPT to Explore Character Backstories and Inner Desires

One of the most magical tools in your Romantasy toolkit isn't a plot twist or a world-shaking spell—it's the truth your characters try to hide. The backstory they avoid. The thing they secretly want more than anything, even if they'd never say it out loud. When your characters have emotional depth, the romance feels real. When they have hidden pain, longing, and fear, readers don't just read your story—they *feel* it.

But building that emotional core can be overwhelming. Especially if you're trying to write fast, or if you have a whole fantasy world to juggle on top of the romance. That's where ChatGPT can become your most intuitive creative partner. Not just for dialogue or plot beats, but for uncovering who your characters *are* beneath the surface.

So let's talk about how to use ChatGPT to dive into your characters' backstories and inner desires, and how that emotional groundwork fuels the heart of your Romantasy.

Let's start with backstory. You don't need to write a full character biography with every childhood event and broken friendship. What you need is to identify the emotional scars and defining choices that shape how your character views love, trust, and power. Ask questions like:

"What moment in their past shaped how they feel about falling in love?"

"Did they have a first love who betrayed them?"

"Were they raised in a family that saw love as weakness?"

"Have they ever chosen duty over desire?"

You can type those questions into ChatGPT, or go even broader:

"Give me five tragic or bittersweet events that could shape the worldview of a Romantasy protagonist who fears intimacy."

"Suggest a backstory for a romantic lead who hides their feelings behind humor."

"What kind of childhood would make someone terrified of being chosen but desperate to be seen?"

What ChatGPT gives you might not be perfect, but you'll almost always find something that clicks—an angle you hadn't considered. Something that *feels* right for the character, even if you tweak the details.

You can also create a conversation between you and your character. Just prompt:

"Pretend you are my Romantasy protagonist. I'm going to ask you questions about your past. Answer in character."

Then type:

"What's something you've never told anyone—not even your love interest?"

"What do you regret most?"

"What scares you about falling in love?"

Watch the answers spill out. You'll be surprised how quickly you start *hearing* your character's voice.

Once you've gotten a grip on the backstory, it's time to explore inner desires. These are different from goals. Goals are what the character *thinks* they want—defeat the villain, protect the kingdom, find the lost relic. But inner desires are emotional. They want to be loved without conditions. To prove they're worthy. To feel safe. To feel powerful. To *belong*.

These desires shape every romantic choice. Maybe the protagonist keeps pushing the love interest away because they believe love always ends in abandonment. Maybe the romantic lead acts distant because they were once manipulated by someone who pretended to care. Maybe the tension isn't about the plot at all—it's about the fact that both characters want to be chosen, but are too scared to ask for it.

Ask ChatGPT for help digging deeper:

"What hidden emotional needs might drive a Romantasy protagonist who's afraid of being vulnerable?"

"List internal desires that could make a magically powerful character feel weak when they fall in love."

"What secret dream might a hardened warrior carry that they never say aloud?"

Even better—explore how *both* characters' inner desires clash or complement each other. Try:

"Describe the emotional dynamic between a Romantasy couple where one character craves control and the other craves freedom."

"Give me relationship tension ideas for two characters who both long for love but are terrified of being truly seen."

These insights help you write scenes with layered subtext. The conversation about the broken charm becomes a conversation about *trust*. The fight about magic is really about *fear of abandonment*. The kiss that doesn't happen? That's the moment they both realize wanting each other means tearing down everything they've built to survive.

The best Romantasy stories don't just have cool powers and epic quests. They have *wounds*. And those wounds don't go away when the characters fall in love—they *flare*. The love interest becomes the mirror. The trigger. The test.

That's where your character work pays off. And the more time you spend asking questions like "What haunts them?" or "What do they need to believe in order to love fully?", the more powerful your emotional beats will be.

Another great exercise: ask ChatGPT to simulate a journal entry or letter from your character.

"Write a private letter from my Romantasy protagonist to their romantic interest that they never send."

"Write a journal entry where they admit how much they want to be loved—but don't think they deserve it."

You'll uncover language you can repurpose later. Maybe an exact line makes its way into a climactic confession. Maybe just the *feeling* of the letter guides a scene's tone. Either way, you're mining emotional gold.

And don't forget—backstory and inner desire don't have to be tragic. Joy can shape someone too. A moment of kindness that changed their life. A fantasy about growing old with someone under a sky of floating lanterns. These small, quiet hopes are often more revealing than the big, dramatic ones. Ask:

"What is something my character secretly hopes for, but would never admit—not even to themselves?"

That's the line you write toward.

In the end, your characters' emotional truths *are* your story. The magic, the setting, the tropes—they all orbit around these hearts. So take the time to listen to them. Let them surprise you. Let ChatGPT help you uncover the layers, then write your scenes from the inside out.

Because when you know what your character truly wants—and what they're afraid it will cost—they'll come alive on the page. And readers will fall for them, just like they fall for each other.

In the next chapter, we'll explore worldbuilding through emotional lenses—how to design a fantasy setting that reflects, challenges, and intensifies the love story you're telling.

Let's build a world that aches with magic.

Worldbuilding with Wonder and Logic

Fantasy worldbuilding can be thrilling... and overwhelming. You've probably got dozens of half-formed ideas floating around—floating cities, magical forests, talking rivers, twin moons, shadow-marked kings. But in Romantasy, your world isn't just there to impress the reader. It's there to *serve the love story*. It should feel like it was built not just for epic moments—but for emotional ones.

So how do you build a world that feels alive, magical, and *logical*—without losing that sense of wonder? How do you avoid getting buried in maps, calendars, and fake histories while still creating a setting that feels *real* enough to fall in love in?

The answer is this: build *emotion first*. Then wrap your logic around it.

Let's start with wonder.

Wonder doesn't come from how many kingdoms or species you invent. It comes from how the world makes your characters feel. The moment they step into the ruins of a lost city and whisper the names of the people who once danced there. The way a lantern spell flickers to life when two hands touch. The scent of magic in the air before a storm. Wonder is built on *sensory detail* and *emotional resonance*. Not just "what is this place?" but "what does it *feel* like to be here?"

Ask yourself questions like:

- What's the most beautiful place in this world, and why does it matter to my characters?
- What place do they go when they want to be alone?
- Where did they first feel magic?
- What's something that *used* to be magical but now isn't?

This will give your world depth *without* needing to explain every system, lineage, or trade route. You're not building a fantasy atlas. You're creating a place where *love can grow*. A place where conflict can spark, where decisions carry weight, and where magic reflects emotion.

Now let's talk logic.

You need just enough rules to make the world *feel* like it runs on something real—even if it's dream logic. For example, if your world has floating cities, how do people get up there? What happens when it rains? If magic is rare, who controls it? What's the cost? You don't need to answer everything. But you *do* need consistency.

Readers will forgive all kinds of fantastical things—talking animals, time loops, soul bonds—*as long as your story plays fair*. That means once you establish a rule, follow it. If love magic only works when both people are honest, then a lie must break it. If a kiss can seal a spell, it can also unseal it. That kind of logic doesn't restrict you—it deepens the drama.

You can use ChatGPT to help structure your world without falling down rabbit holes. Ask:

"Suggest three magical cultures that reflect different attitudes toward love and power."

"Give me a list of magical locations that could mirror emotional turning points in a Romantasy novel."

"Help me invent a myth that explains how magic and romance became connected in this world."

What you're doing here is *anchoring emotion to environment.* That's what makes Romantasy special. The world doesn't just exist in the background—it *responds* to the story. If your characters are falling apart, maybe the land is falling into decay too. If they finally come together, maybe the long-dead roses start to bloom again. Let the world echo the love.

Want to build social structures that influence romance? Great. Maybe in this world, magical marriage bonds are unbreakable. Maybe bloodlines are preserved through arranged soul pairings. Maybe kissing is a sacred ritual—and your characters do it by accident. Or maybe love is outlawed because it causes uncontrollable magic surges. These are cultural rules that create conflict and stakes for your romance.

Logic gives you limits. And in storytelling, limits are good. Limits force choices. Choices drive emotion.

You also want to think about how people *live* in this world. What do they wear? Eat? Fear? Celebrate? You don't need to write ten pages about it—but if you know the basics, you can color your scenes with texture. Maybe magic-users have a scent—like ozone or lilies. Maybe townsfolk hang bells on their doors to ward off heartbreak spells. Maybe every year there's a Moonfall festival where everyone wears masks, and your characters kiss without knowing each other's identities.

These little details make your world feel *true.* They give readers something to dream about, something to feel grounded in, even as they soar.

Here's a trick: worldbuild *through your characters' eyes.* Don't start with the universe. Start with what your protagonist believes. What did they grow up thinking magic was? How did they see love modeled—or not? What places scare them? What places make them feel safe?

From there, build outward. If your main character is terrified of falling in love because they saw it destroy someone, then maybe your world has a legend about a love so powerful it tore two continents apart. That's worldbuilding in service of *emotion*. That's how you keep it focused and meaningful.

One more trick: don't be afraid to withhold information. Mystery creates wonder. Maybe your characters don't *know* how the magic works. Maybe nobody does. Maybe your world has forgotten its origins, and rediscovering that truth is part of the journey. Not every rule needs to be explained in the first few chapters. Let the reader discover the world as the characters do—through need, emotion, and conflict.

If you get stuck, tell ChatGPT:

"Help me design a magical forest that reflects grief and healing."

"Describe a city where love is currency and magic is traded through memories."

"Suggest worldbuilding ideas based on a Romantasy theme of sacrifice."

You'll get inspired not just by places, but by *possibilities*.

Ultimately, worldbuilding in Romantasy is less about building a perfect system and more about crafting an environment that heightens the love story. A world where kissing someone could light up the sky—or end the world. A world where falling in love isn't just dangerous—it's revolutionary.

So ask yourself: what kind of world would *only* exist to challenge, reveal, and transform these two people?

Then build that.

Inventing Fantasy Cultures, Creatures, and Customs That Shape Love

When you're writing a Romantasy, love doesn't happen in a vacuum. It's shaped by the world it grows in—by culture, by beliefs, by strange creatures who might understand emotion differently, by traditions and taboos that twist desire into something forbidden or fated. The beauty of Romantasy is that you're not writing about just any kind of love. You're writing about love that blooms in impossible places, under impossible rules, and sometimes *because* of them.

So if you want your world to feel alive, don't just build kingdoms and climates. Build *love systems*. Cultural norms, magical creatures, and emotional rituals that influence how people give and receive affection. That's what makes the story feel like it couldn't exist anywhere else.

Let's start with culture. In your fantasy world, what is love *supposed* to look like? Is it arranged and strategic, or passionate and messy? Is it something hidden or something celebrated? Do people choose partners freely, or are their matches written in stars, dreams, or bloodlines? Are there contracts, enchantments, or trials before one can say "I love you"?

Ask yourself:

- What's the biggest love taboo in this society?
- What's the grandest gesture of devotion?
- How do people say "I love you" without words?
- What stories do children grow up hearing about love?

You don't need to write a full anthropology textbook. One or two well-placed customs can flavor your entire world. Maybe in one kingdom, couples carve their names into each other's shadows during a moonless night. Maybe in another, magical rings bind emotions until one is removed—and removing it is a betrayal. These aren't just cool ideas. They're *story fuel.*

Use ChatGPT to brainstorm quickly:

"Invent five fantasy wedding rituals that involve magic and sacrifice."

"What kind of love customs might develop in a desert culture where water is sacred?"

"Suggest romantic taboos in a society where people are bonded by shared dreams."

Even a single answer can spark a whole subplot or shift the meaning of a scene.

Now let's talk about creatures. Fantasy worlds are full of non-human beings, and this is where you can get truly creative. These creatures don't just have to be enemies or background scenery. They can be deeply entwined with the emotional fabric of your story.

What if there are mythical animals that only appear when two people fall in love? What if certain beings feed on longing or protect those with broken hearts? What if dragons mate for life—and this bond is revered, feared, or mimicked by the people who live near them?

You can also flip the lens. What if your romantic lead *isn't* human? How do they experience love? How do they interpret gestures like touch, scent, or sound? Maybe they don't understand monogamy. Maybe they bond through magic, not words. That disconnect can lead to fascinating tension—and intense character growth.

Ask ChatGPT:

"Create a fantasy creature that reacts to emotional energy and appears during heartbreak."

"Describe a sentient magical species whose courtship involves sharing memories."

"Invent a legend about a creature whose song causes people to fall in love or remember lost love."

These creatures don't just add depth—they *shift the rules*. They change what's possible. And that forces your characters to respond, adapt, and evolve.

Customs are the third ingredient, and they're where culture and creatures collide. They're the day-to-day stuff that makes your world feel lived in. Not just what love means *in theory*, but how it's practiced. Do people give tokens of affection? Leave offerings? Sing spells? Write names in salt? What holidays or festivals bring people together—or push them apart?

Let's say your world has a winter festival where people wear masks and ask strangers to dance. That could lead to a love story full of hidden identities, longing, and mistaken choices. Or maybe the culture believes in "soul-flares," where once in a person's life, they're struck by a sudden magical surge when they meet their true match—and must choose whether to follow it or walk away. The possibilities are endless.

A few strong customs, used well, can completely shape your characters' worldview. If your protagonist comes from a culture where love is tied to loyalty and public service, they might struggle to understand the romantic lead who comes from a place where passion is private and fleeting. That clash? That's where story happens.

Even better, you can show love *changing* these customs. Maybe two characters from rival nations forge a new ritual together—one that blends both cultures. Maybe their bond challenges an old law or breaks a sacred tradition. Suddenly, love isn't just emotional—it's *revolutionary*.

This is the beauty of Romantasy: love doesn't just live in the heart. It moves through magic, politics, myth, and culture. It causes ripple effects. It disrupts. It transforms.

If you're writing quickly and don't want to invent everything from scratch, you can use ChatGPT like a cultural generator:

"What love traditions might exist in a mountain society that worships silence?"

"Invent a festival for forbidden lovers to meet in secret."

"Describe an ancient prophecy about a pair of soul-bound warriors who must never touch."

Let your AI partner throw ideas at you. Even if you change them, even if you twist them beyond recognition, they'll give you ground to stand on—and stories to chase.

At the end of the day, cultures, creatures, and customs aren't just worldbuilding details. They're emotional tools. They show us what love looks like when it's filtered through fear, ritual, duty, magic, and myth. They tell us what your characters have to *overcome* to be together. What they'll risk. What they'll change.

And when they finally kiss—under the wrong moon, in defiance of an ancient law, with a dragon circling overhead and magic surging through their veins—it won't just be romantic. It'll be *earned*.

Building Magical Places for Romance to Bloom (or Explode)

Some stories take place. Others *feel* like a place. In Romantasy, the setting isn't just a backdrop—it's an accomplice. A partner in the romance. A mood. A pressure point. The right magical place can turn a quiet confession into a legendary moment—or make a kiss feel like the start of a war. You don't need a dozen countries or endless maps. You need a few vivid, emotionally charged locations where love either *blooms* or *detonates*.

These are the places readers remember long after the plot fades. The moonlit ruins where two rivals almost kiss. The enchanted glade where someone first hears "I love you." The cliff's edge where betrayal and desire meet in the same heartbeat. Settings in Romantasy are more than geography. They're *emotional stages*—designed for specific kinds of transformation.

Let's start with romantic settings that help love bloom.

Think about intimacy. Secrecy. Stillness. These are places where the outside world pauses just long enough for hearts to speak. That could be a magical garden that only opens to soulmates. A cave lit by glowing moss that warms as people speak the truth. A tower where time slows down, giving the couple space to connect. These aren't just pretty—they create *emotional permission*. They allow softness, vulnerability, hesitation.

What makes a location romantic in fantasy isn't just the flowers and stars—it's what the place *protects the characters from*. These spots are refuges. Temporary safe zones. They contrast with the conflict outside. Even if danger looms, these places are the eye of the storm.

Now flip it. What about locations where romance *explodes*?

These are pressure-cooker settings. Charged. Dangerous. Full of distraction, temptation, risk. Think of a royal ballroom where dancing together is a political statement. A battlefield where saving someone becomes an act of love. A cursed library where passion and fear blur together. These are places where emotions *can't be contained*—where whatever your characters have been trying to hide finally bursts out.

Romantic tension thrives in environments that either trap or isolate. A magical blizzard that strands two enemies. A bonding ritual they must complete *together*, even as they try to resist it. A masquerade where truths are spoken under false names. The setting becomes the *accelerant*. It speeds up everything your characters are trying to slow down.

You can even create locations that are *alive*—that respond to emotion. Maybe the ground blooms when they touch. Maybe lights flicker during tension. Maybe the entire forest holds its breath during a kiss. This kind of environmental magic blurs the line between setting and mood, making your world feel like it's conspiring with the romance.

Don't forget how memory attaches to place. The first time your characters kiss? That setting becomes charged forever. The next time they return, the emotional weight has changed. Maybe it used to be safety. Now it's sorrow. Maybe it used to be forbidden. Now it's sacred. Revisiting places after key romantic moments gives your world emotional layering—and makes readers ache.

If you're not sure what kind of setting a scene needs, ask yourself:

- Is this a moment of tension or release?
- Do the characters need privacy, pressure, or both?

- What would make this setting *impossible to forget*?

Then build around that. Don't be afraid to tie your locations to *themes*. If your story is about transformation, create places where the land is constantly shifting—forests that re-grow, cities that appear at night, floating temples. If your story is about forbidden love, use borderlands, shadow realms, or locked rooms. Make the setting *echo the stakes*.

ChatGPT can help brainstorm endlessly here. Try prompts like:

"Create a romantic fantasy setting where time behaves strangely."

"Describe a cursed lake where lovers go to say goodbye."

"Invent a secret place where two rival heirs meet in secret."

You'll get ideas you can bend, merge, or twist to fit your world—and your emotional beats.

Also think small. You don't need giant magical landscapes to make a scene unforgettable. A single room can carry the entire weight of your romance. A doorway. A stairwell. A bathhouse. A tent. A cell. A rooftop under falling stardust. It's not about scope—it's about *intensity*. A kiss in a forgotten hallway can be more powerful than one on a mountaintop, if the emotions are right. Don't be afraid to contrast setting with emotion. Sometimes the sweetest love scene happens in the middle of chaos. Sometimes a bitter breakup happens in the prettiest place in the world. That tension between what the world looks like and what the characters feel? That's magic.

You can also reverse-engineer moments from places. Instead of starting with "I want them to kiss," start with "What's a place where kissing would be *dangerous, thrilling, and completely unexpected*?" Let the location *decide* the emotion. That often leads to surprises—for you and the reader. Lastly, think about how your characters relate to these places. Is there somewhere one of them refuses to go? A place they dreamed of showing someone they love? A location they only enter when they're falling apart? These kinds of associations give the world personal meaning. And when that place is finally shared with someone else—especially the love interest—it hits harder.

Because in Romantasy, place is never just place. It's memory. It's desire. It's the quiet echo of all the things left unsaid.

So build your magical world not as a map, but as a *mood-board of emotion*. Fill it with places where your characters collide, open up, fall apart, and try again. Places that remember. Places that forgive. Places that burn.

Writing Dialogue That Feels Alive, Not Expository

Nothing kills the magic of Romantasy faster than dialogue that feels like a plot summary wearing a costume. You know the kind—lines where the characters are clearly just there to explain the world, the backstory, the curse, the plan, the magic system, the political situation, and the prophecy... all in one breath. It's like the romance has to pause so the world can catch up. But that's not how real people talk, and it's definitely not how characters fall in love.

In Romantasy, your dialogue should *spark*, *sting*, *flirt*, and *reveal*. It should feel like a dance—sometimes hesitant, sometimes confrontational, often layered with subtext. It should sound like your characters are breathing, not briefing.

So let's talk about how to write dialogue that feels alive. That pulls readers closer instead of pushing them out with exposition. That builds romance, tension, world, and character all at once—without ever feeling like a lecture.

First, understand this: good dialogue doesn't explain—it *exposes*. It shows us who your characters are through what they say, how they say it, what they choose *not* to say, and what slips out by accident. You can give us worldbuilding details through dialogue, but they should come from a place of emotion, not obligation.

Instead of this:

"As you know, Prince Thane, the Bloodbound are forbidden from entering the Temple of Echoes without an oath of silence, and your father died trying to defy that law."

Try this:

"Go ahead. Walk in. Your father did too. They're still scraping pieces of him off the walls."

See the difference? One tells us facts. The other gives us *character*. Attitude. History. Tension. And we still learn the same thing—but we *feel* it now.

If you need to drop information, wrap it in conflict or emotion. People don't recite facts in real life—they use information to accuse, deflect, warn, seduce, or survive. So should your characters.

Now let's bring it closer to romance.

Romantic dialogue shouldn't always be smooth. Sometimes it's awkward. Sometimes it's heated. Sometimes it's two people saying anything but what they actually mean. The best romantic lines are often disguised as insults, deflections, or dry humor. Don't force your characters to say "I love you" on page thirty. Let them *fight* that feeling. Let them speak through metaphor, implication, silence.

Think of a line like:

"If you die, I will raise you from the dead just so I can kill you myself."

That's a threat. But it's also a *declaration*. And it's way more interesting than a plain "Don't die."

Use contrast in your dialogue. A snarky character might go quiet when the moment gets tender. A stoic type might suddenly spill something too honest and then pretend it didn't happen. Play with those moments where words come too easily—or not at all.

You can also build romance through repetition and callbacks. Maybe the love interest always says "You don't scare me" in response to danger. Then, in a moment of vulnerability, they say it when looking directly into the protagonist's eyes. That shift? That's character arc through dialogue. No info dump needed.

If your dialogue feels flat, try stripping it back. People rarely speak in full sentences or formal language unless they're nervous, angry, or hiding something. Let characters interrupt each other. Trail off. Say something stupid and regret it. One half-sentence can carry more weight than a paragraph of explanation if the timing and tension are right.

You can use ChatGPT to help develop sharper dialogue. Try prompts like:

"Write a romantic argument between two characters who are pretending not to be in love."

"Give me ten flirtatious lines a morally gray character might say to someone they care about but won't admit it."

"Write dialogue between two characters discussing a magical curse they both know is slowly binding them together."

These kinds of prompts can help you unlock tone, rhythm, and character voice. You don't have to use the lines exactly—just borrow the energy.

Another great trick: rewrite a flat exchange in multiple emotional modes.

Let's say your characters are talking about a dangerous mission. Try writing the same dialogue as:

- a flirtation
- a bitter argument
- a confessional
- a joke
- a power play

This shows you all the different *ways* dialogue can function in the same scene. Then choose the one that fits the relationship best—or creates the most delicious tension.

Also, think of how your fantasy world might shape language. Are there specific words only used in romantic bonds? Do curses get thrown around during intimacy? Are there magical phrases too dangerous to say unless you mean them? Build culture and magic *into* your dialogue. Don't explain them—let them *exist* in how people talk. The more confident your characters are in their world, the more real it will feel to your reader.

Dialogue also builds pacing. A sharp, rapid-fire exchange can ramp up tension. A slow, breathy scene with minimal words can let emotion simmer. You don't need long speeches to make a moment powerful. Sometimes it's just:

"You're shaking."

"I'm not afraid."

"Then what are you?"

"Yours."

Boom. Four lines. A whole turning point.

And if you need to sneak in exposition? Do it through *conflict or comedy*. Sarcastic characters are great at this. They can throw a ton of information at the reader in a single rant or complaint, and it feels natural. Same with power struggles—characters arguing about history, magic laws, family drama. Just keep the emotions front and center. The facts will follow.

Finally, let your characters sound *different* from each other. Give them individual rhythms, vocab, favorite phrases. One character might ramble. Another might only speak when cornered. One might swear like it's a second language. Another might quote poetry without realizing it. Those choices make your dialogue sparkle—and make your characters unforgettable.

Language of Love: Metaphors, Similes, and Sensual Descriptions

In Romantasy, the heart speaks in magic—but the *words* still matter. What your characters say and how you describe what they feel can either sweep your reader into the moment or flatten it entirely. You're not just writing about a kiss, a touch, a look—you're writing about the *feeling of it*, the heat behind it, the way it lingers in the blood or settles in the bones. To do that, you need the tools of figurative language: metaphors, similes, and sensory details that don't just describe the moment—they *transform* it.

Let's be clear: love is rarely just "his lips on hers" or "her heart beating fast." That's not bad, it's just... not enough. In Romantasy, you have the chance to make love feel like lightning, like prophecy, like danger and warmth in the same breath. You have permission to go *poetic*. In fact, your readers want it.

So let's talk about how to use metaphors, similes, and sensual description in a way that elevates your prose but keeps it honest—never purple, never forced, always grounded in character and emotion.

Start with *emotion before action*.

Don't describe the kiss first. Describe the build-up. Describe what it feels like to *almost* kiss. What it costs. What's at stake. Metaphors are most powerful in those moments of hesitation and want.

"Her gaze hit him like a secret he wasn't supposed to know."

"His name burned in her mouth like a spell she was too afraid to speak."

See how the metaphor goes beyond just description? It captures internal state. It gives weight to the moment.

And then, when the physical act comes—make it specific. Not just "he touched her face," but:

"His fingers traced her jaw like he was trying to memorize a constellation."

You're not trying to describe *exactly* what's happening—you're describing what it *feels like* to the character. That's the goal.

Similes bring clarity through comparison.

A simile says "this is like that," and it can bring emotional resonance quickly.

"Her smile was like the first fire after a long winter."

"He held her like he was afraid the air would steal her away."

These paint a picture. They connect readers to something familiar, something visceral. But keep similes tight and purposeful. If the image doesn't serve a feeling or make the moment sharper, cut it.

Avoid tired comparisons. If her heart is "beating like a drum" or his eyes are "blue like the sea," that's fine—but it's also forgettable. Push yourself further. If her heart is beating like a war anthem, or like a hummingbird in a storm, that's something we haven't quite heard before.

Use the *senses*—but not just the obvious ones.

Yes, touch is key in Romantasy. But don't forget about sound, scent, taste, and even temperature. A love scene becomes immersive when it goes beyond skin.

"The warmth of her skin made the cold air ache against his neck."

"His voice, low and raw, sounded like something pulled from the bottom of a well."

"The air between them tasted like smoke and moonlight—sharp, impossible."

That last one? It doesn't make literal sense, but it *feels* right. That's the power of sensual description—it isn't about being realistic. It's about being *felt*.

Be aware of rhythm.

Your sentences should move like your characters do. Fast, clipped lines for urgency and tension. Long, flowing sentences for tenderness or intoxication.

A kiss written in short bursts feels panicked, hungry:

"She leaned in. Stopped. He was too close. Too far. Her breath hitched. His hand trembled."

Now compare that to:

"Their mouths met slowly, like a spell unraveling, like the world had decided to pause and listen."

See how the rhythm changes the mood?

When writing about passion or emotional vulnerability, think like a composer. Let the structure of your sentences *carry* the tension.

Don't overwrite.

Yes, this chapter is about using poetic language. But too much can dull the blade. If every line is a metaphor, none of them will land. You need contrast—some clean, grounded sentences so that the lyrical ones *shine*. Give readers space to breathe.

Sometimes the most powerful line is the simplest:

"She didn't want to let go."

"He couldn't look at her and still lie."

Let those moments sit next to the more poetic ones. They'll strengthen each other.

Let the metaphors grow with the story.

If your protagonist first describes the love interest as "a storm on the horizon," and then later describes them as "the eye of the storm," that's not just nice wordplay—it's *narrative evolution*. You're showing us how feelings change, deepen, shift.

Maybe the first time they touch, it's described as "heat." Later, "gravity." Finally, "home." That's arc. That's development. That's prose working in harmony with plot.

Use ChatGPT to help stretch your imagery.

Try prompts like:

"Give me metaphors for love that feel dangerous and magical."

"Write similes describing the moment before a kiss in a fantasy setting."

"Suggest sensual descriptions that don't rely on clichés like 'heart pounding' or 'weak at the knees.'"

You'll be surprised by the sparks this can generate. Even if none of the examples are perfect, they'll push you out of your usual phrasing. They'll stretch your language muscles.

And when you find one that lands? It will stick with your readers for *chapters*.

One last thing: tie your figurative language to your world.

If your world is built around moon magic, maybe love glows, waxes, wanes. If your magic is tied to threads or weaving, maybe kisses feel like knots pulling tight. If love in your world is considered dangerous, let the metaphors be edged—iron, fire, poison, battle.

This anchors the romance to the setting. It makes your story feel like it could *only* happen here.

Because in Romantasy, we're not just reading about people falling in love. We're reading about *what it feels like* to fall in love in a world built to test, elevate, and challenge every feeling.

So use your language like a spell. Let it tingle. Let it sting. Let it say what the characters won't.

Using Symbolism to Deepen Romance and Theme

In Romantasy, the deepest love stories aren't just told through kisses and confessions. They're whispered through objects, echoed in imagery, and repeated in symbols that seem small at first—until they mean everything. Symbolism is the secret layer of meaning that turns a pretty story into a powerful one. It weaves theme and romance together in a way readers may not always notice consciously, but they'll *feel* it. It's what makes a scene resonate long after it's over. A necklace, a broken sword, a shared flower, a shadow on the wall—when done right, these things become *emotional landmarks*.

So let's talk about how to use symbolism in your Romantasy without it feeling like homework. How do you make it feel like a natural part of the story rather than a literary trick? How do you embed meaning without shouting, "Hey, this is important!"

Start with this idea: a symbol is just *a thing that means more than it should*. That's it. It could be a color, a place, a gesture, a sound, a season, a magical element, an animal, an object—literally anything. What makes it powerful is that you repeat it. You associate it with an emotion. And you let it evolve.

Let's say your protagonist always wears a red scarf. At first, it's just something they stole. Later, we find out it belonged to their brother who died protecting them. Then, in a key romantic moment, the love interest touches the scarf—gently—and says nothing. Now it's no longer just fabric. It's *trust*. It's memory. It's grief. And when that scarf is left behind or burned or given away? That moment *hurts*.

That's how symbols work. You take something ordinary and make it emotionally loaded through context and repetition.

In Romantasy, symbolism can connect to both love and theme at once. For example, if your story's about sacrifice, maybe you use mirrors as a recurring symbol—because mirrors show the self, and your characters keep having to choose someone else over their reflection. Maybe every time they look into a mirror, they see more of who they don't want to be. Until finally, they shatter one. Or turn away. That's theme and emotion woven together—quietly, beautifully.

Now think about your world. What are the magical or cultural symbols that already exist? Can you tie them to romance? Maybe two soul-bound people share matching marks that only glow when they're near each other—but the marks flicker whenever they lie. Maybe certain flowers bloom only for people who are truly in love, so someone faking it would never dare to send a bouquet. Maybe there's a tradition of gifting feathers during courtship, but your character—who doesn't believe in love—gives one anyway. That gesture, small on the surface, can *wreck* a reader who knows what it means.

Use ChatGPT to help build some of these ideas:

"Suggest symbolic objects in a Romantasy story that could represent hidden love."

"Give me five nature-based symbols that could be tied to emotional growth and romance."

"What kinds of cultural symbols might exist in a fantasy world where love is rare or sacred?"

Even better, ask for the *evolution* of a symbol:

"Describe how a gemstone given as a gift could change meaning over the course of a love story—from protection, to control, to freedom."

Let's talk about gesture-based symbolism too. Maybe your characters always say goodbye with a hand over the heart. Maybe they light candles for each other in secret. Maybe every time they touch, it's the same hand, the same pressure—until it changes. These kinds of symbols don't require explanation. The reader picks them up naturally through repetition.

One of the most powerful symbolic arcs you can write is when something goes from neutral to meaningful. Maybe it's a dagger one character gives the other "just in case." But that dagger ends up saving a life, or being used to betray, or being left behind as a message. The reader goes, "Oh. *That* dagger." And they *feel* something.

Symbolism is especially potent when you layer it in visually. Fantasy gives you lush imagery to work with—moons, stars, light, shadow, blood, flowers, ash. These aren't just pretty. They carry mood. Think of how often roses are used to represent both beauty and danger. What if, in your world, roses only bloom where someone has made a vow they cannot keep? Suddenly, your love scene in a rose garden has teeth.

Or say your story has a lot of water-based imagery. Maybe your theme is emotional control versus surrender. You could build that out symbolically. The protagonist avoids water, is afraid of it. The love interest swims, surfs, controls storms. The final romantic moment? The protagonist walks into the ocean willingly—for the first time.

That's not a monologue. That's *symbolic payoff.*

Don't force it. But do plan it. If you find a symbol early in your story, make a note to bring it back later with a twist. Maybe something that represented hope in Act One becomes a sign of regret in Act Three. Or something they dismissed as superstition ends up being the very thing that saves them—because they learned to believe. That growth, symbolized through an object or image, becomes *emotionally amplified.*

A quick list of symbol types to explore:

- **Colors**: White for forgetting, gold for fate, blue for longing.
- **Elements**: Fire for passion or destruction, water for change, earth for protection.
- **Animals**: Crows for warning, wolves for loyalty, butterflies for transformation.
- **Rituals**: Lighting a lantern, tying a cord, leaving something behind.
- **Weather**: Storms for emotional turmoil, fog for confusion, snow for clarity or quiet.

Tie these to character moments and watch your scenes deepen.

One last tip: not everything symbolic has to be explained. In fact, the best ones rarely are. Let the reader make the connection. Let them feel smart, feel involved, feel part of the world. They'll thank you for it with tears, gasps, and fan art.

Symbolism, when used with care, makes your story feel like it matters more. Like it meant something *before* it started and will mean something *after* it ends. It gives readers something to hold onto. A thread of meaning to follow. A sign they missed the first time that suddenly lights up everything.

Flashbacks, Dreams, and Prophecies: The Past as Emotional Weight

In Romantasy, the past isn't gone. It's *haunting*. It lingers like the echo of a spell long broken—or one still waiting to be fulfilled. Whether it comes in the form of a flashback, a dream, or a prophecy, the past holds emotional weight that deepens the present. It's not just backstory. It's subtext. It's fuel. It's the reason your characters flinch before they kiss, or hesitate before they trust, or carry a blade they swore never to use again.

Using flashbacks, dreams, and prophecies isn't just about showing what happened or what might happen. It's about layering meaning. It's about using time—bent and broken—as a mirror for your characters' inner lives. And in Romantasy, where love and fate are often intertwined, the past can feel as alive as any dragon, curse, or kingdom.

Let's start with **flashbacks**.

These aren't info dumps. A flashback, done right, is like memory bleeding into the story. It's an interruption—soft or jarring—that reveals something your character hasn't said out loud. It's the moment they touched a grave and remembered the day they lost their sibling. The time they tried to confess love and were met with silence. The oath they took, not fully understanding what it would cost.

A great flashback is emotionally charged and short. It drops into the scene like a heartbeat skipping—then fades. Think of it like an emotional punch, not a history lesson.

Instead of:

"She remembered training as a child with her aunt in the Temple of Glass, where she learned to use blood magic and was warned never to fall in love."

Try:

"The scent of jasmine made her flinch. It had always clung to her aunt's robes, the night she whispered, 'Love makes you weak. That's how they'll break you.'"

Suddenly, the past is speaking to the present. That's how you use flashback as emotional weight.

Now let's talk **dreams**.

Fantasy and dreams are natural companions. But dreams in Romantasy aren't just surreal or poetic—they're usually *warning signs, reflections, or repressed desires*. They allow your characters to experience truths they're not ready to face consciously. Maybe your protagonist dreams of their love interest dying—again and again—and can't understand why it feels like memory. Maybe the romantic lead dreams of their soulmate every night but never sees their face—until the first kiss, when the dream changes.

You don't need to explain how dreams work in your world. Just use them carefully. Dream scenes should reveal something real. Fear, longing, a glimpse of fate. And sometimes, a lie. What matters most is how your character feels *after* the dream.

A good dream scene might look like this:

"He woke with her name in his mouth and the taste of lightning on his tongue. He didn't know why, but his hands were shaking—and the fire at the hearth had died."

There's tension. There's confusion. And there's symbolic residue. The dream has done its job.

Use ChatGPT to generate dream sequences that resonate:

"Write a dream for a Romantasy character who's afraid of falling in love but already has."

"Describe a recurring dream that hints at a forgotten past life romance."

"Suggest a symbolic dream for a character with repressed magic linked to their feelings."

Dreams are emotional x-rays. Let them show what the character doesn't even know they're carrying.

Finally, let's explore **prophecies**.

Romantasy loves a good prophecy. The chosen one. The forbidden love. The tragic ending foretold. But prophecy can be a trap if it's too rigid or too convenient. The key is to use it not as a rulebook—but as *pressure*. A prophecy shouldn't feel like a script. It should feel like a *burden*. Something your characters try to avoid, deny, challenge, or fear. That tension between fate and free will? That's where the magic lives.

Maybe the prophecy says your protagonist will destroy the one they love. Maybe it says they *must* marry someone they haven't met yet. Maybe it says nothing at all—just a vague phrase like, "The heart that bleeds for the crown will drown the kingdom in light."

Let the prophecy be interpreted, misread, misunderstood. Let your characters believe they're defying it—until they realize they're walking straight into its teeth.

And if you're feeling clever, you can make the prophecy emotional rather than plot-based. Instead of "You will save the world," try:

"You will not be loved until you let go of your first grief."

Now the character's journey becomes an internal one. The prophecy is still driving the story, but it's doing so through the heart.

Want to brainstorm prophecies with ChatGPT? Try:

"Invent a prophecy for a Romantasy story where love is forbidden by magical law."

"Write a poetic prophecy that hints at two lovers who will break the cycle of war."

"Suggest cryptic lines for a Romantasy prophecy that can be interpreted multiple ways."

Once you have your prophecy, flashbacks and dreams can start to swirl around it. The past offers clues. The dreams offer feelings. The prophecy offers stakes.

The key is this: don't treat flashbacks, dreams, and prophecies as detours. They are *emotional accelerators*. They let your readers feel the full *weight* of a decision before your character even knows they have to make it. Because in Romantasy, the past isn't just a story behind the story—it's a *shadow cast over the future*. The heartbreak that already happened. The love that never got a chance. The promise made lifetimes ago that still hasn't been fulfilled. Use that shadow well, and every kiss will feel deeper. Every confession will feel earned. Every act of love will carry the ache of everything that came before.

Weaving Subplots: Side Quests, Secret Lovers, and Rivalries

Romantasy may be a love story at heart, but it's rarely just a straight line from "I hate you" to "I love you." The magic of this genre often lies in what's happening *around* the central romance—the side quests, secret lovers, rivalries, betrayals, friendships, and hidden motivations that pull the characters away from each other just as often as they draw them close. These subplots are the lifeblood of your world. They add texture, create momentum, and make your story feel rich and lived-in. Without them, the romance has nothing to push against. No friction. No threat. No tension.

And let's be honest: Romantasy readers love a good side tangle. The ex-lover turned enemy. The sibling keeping a magical secret. The loyal friend who might be in love too. The mission that has nothing to do with romance—until it *does.*

So how do you weave subplots into your story in a way that supports the romance without stealing the spotlight? You start by asking: what makes this subplot emotionally *relevant* to the main characters?

Let's break it down.

Side quests

Side quests are perfect for building character and world. They offer your protagonists the chance to show what they value, what they fear, and how they react when things don't go as planned. A mission to retrieve a magical relic? Great. But if it forces the romantic leads to travel together—and sleep two feet apart in a wind-wracked cave—that's even better. Now the quest becomes about *proximity.* About revealing secrets. About slow-burn tension or unresolved anger.

Or maybe the side quest separates them—on purpose. One character is sent to parley with a rival kingdom, while the other stays behind to defend the border. The distance becomes part of the story. The longing. The risk of growing apart. The worry that they'll change—or worse, bond with someone else.

Use ChatGPT to brainstorm mission-based subplots with emotional potential:

"Give me five fantasy side quests that would force two romantic leads to work together despite not trusting each other."

"Suggest a subplot where a solo mission causes one romantic lead to doubt the other's loyalty."

"Describe a magical side quest that brings a buried secret to the surface."

You'll discover that side quests are never just about the task—they're about what happens *between* the steps.

Secret lovers

There's nothing quite like forbidden love to up the stakes. Maybe your protagonist's friend is secretly in love with someone from a rival faction. Or maybe *they* are—on the side. Or maybe they *used to be,* and it's not as over as they pretend. These subplots add layers of emotional conflict. They complicate alliances. They raise questions of loyalty and betrayal.

Secret lovers can also mirror or contrast your central romance. If your main love story is slow-burn and agonizing, the secret romance might be impulsive, doomed, or purely physical. Watching those threads twist together (or unravel) makes the main love story feel *bigger,* by comparison.

Better yet, what if one of your main characters is *part* of a secret romance—or forced into one due to a magical contract, political arrangement, or survival pact? Suddenly, the central romance isn't just about feelings. It's about *risking everything* for those feelings.

Use ChatGPT to sketch out possibilities:

"Suggest five secret romance subplots that would emotionally affect the main romantic leads in a Romantasy novel."

"What are some reasons a character might hide a magical love bond from everyone, even their closest friend?"

"Describe a subplot where a past lover resurfaces and challenges the new romance."

These threads don't need full arcs. Just enough tension to rattle the central relationship. That's what makes them matter.

Rivalries

Enemies make everything better. Especially in Romantasy. A good rival doesn't just oppose your protagonist—they *reflect* something about them. Their ambition. Their fear. Their weakness. A rival might be in love with the same person. Or might represent the life your character could've had, if they'd chosen differently. Or maybe they want power—and think your protagonist's heart is in the way.

Rivalries also allow you to explore different *ideologies*. One character believes love is strength. The rival thinks it's distraction. One thinks magic should be shared. The other believes it should be hoarded. These clashes create stakes not just in action scenes, but in *every* interaction.

And sometimes, the rival becomes a love interest. Or a reluctant ally. Or worse—*a friend who becomes a rival after falling for the same person*. The emotional possibilities are endless.

ChatGPT can help you craft complex opponents:

"Create a rival for a Romantasy protagonist who is both an obstacle and a reflection of their deepest fear."

"Suggest a subplot where a rival becomes unexpectedly sympathetic, forcing the protagonist to question everything."

"What are some rivalries in Romantasy stories that eventually turn romantic?"

Even if your rival stays in their lane, they still help define the emotional stakes. If the lovers fail, *this* person wins. Or survives. Or claims the power. That tension keeps the central romance taut.

Tying it all together

The trick with subplots isn't quantity—it's *interconnection*. The best subplots don't live on the sidelines. They weave through the main plot like vines. Each one should do at least one of the following:

- Reveal something about a main character
- Put emotional pressure on the romance
- Reflect or contrast the central theme
- Raise the stakes, even if only subtly
- Offer a payoff later that deepens the main arc

For example, a side character's forbidden romance could teach the protagonist something about bravery. A rivalry over a magical artifact might force the lovers into temporary opposition. A failed side quest could drive one character into the arms of someone else—if only briefly.

These aren't distractions. They're accelerants. They make the main romance burn brighter.

And don't worry about wrapping every subplot up in a bow. Some are meant to end messily. A betrayal. A goodbye. A relationship that never fully resolves. That kind of open-ended emotion can make your world feel more real—and give your main story sharper edges.

If you're plotting and feel overwhelmed, ask ChatGPT for help with integrating everything:

"Outline a Romantasy story with a central romance, one side quest, one secret lover subplot, and one personal rivalry."

"How could a failed side quest and a secret romance affect the main character's ability to trust?"

"Suggest a final scene where all three subplots come to a head emotionally."

The point isn't to create chaos. It's to create *depth*. Let your story feel crowded with feeling. Let your characters carry more than just one kind of love. More than just one kind of loyalty.

Because in the end, a Romantasy story with strong subplots isn't just about whether the two main characters fall in love. It's about whether they do so *despite* everything else pulling them apart.

When the Fantasy Is a Metaphor for Emotional Growth

One of the most powerful things Romantasy can do is let readers *feel* the truth of something through metaphor—without needing to say it outright. When magic, curses, realms, or fantastical elements act as mirrors for emotional transformation, you're no longer just telling a story about falling in love or fighting a monster. You're telling a story about *healing, letting go, becoming whole,* or *daring to be vulnerable.* And that's when your story goes from fun... to unforgettable.

Let's get this out of the way early: your fantasy doesn't *have* to be a metaphor. Sometimes magic is just magic, and that's totally okay. But when you want your romance to go deeper—when you want to write something that resonates on an almost mythic level—you can use the fantasy elements not just as cool set dressing, but as symbols for what your characters are *emotionally experiencing.*

When done well, your readers may not even realize it consciously. They'll just feel it. A sense that the world and the characters are speaking the same language. That everything—from the glowing sword to the shrinking forest—is part of the same internal journey.

Let's look at some examples of how fantasy can become metaphor:

Maybe your protagonist has buried their grief so deep that it's become a literal curse—one that turns their touch to ice. They don't want to hurt anyone, so they don't let anyone close. Enter the love interest, who isn't afraid to get frostbitten. The "magic problem" isn't just a fantasy mechanic—it's a metaphor for emotional distance. For guilt. For fear of connection. And when they finally learn to let go, the frost melts. Not just because the plot demanded it, but because *they changed.*

That's fantasy as emotional growth.

Or imagine a magical forest that responds to emotion—growing wild and dark when your characters lie, blooming with light when they speak their truth. The world *reflects* their internal state. If they deny their feelings, the forest becomes impossible to pass through. When they finally confess love, the trees part. That's not just beautiful—it's meaningful.

You're telling a love story not just between two people, but between *who they were* and *who they're becoming.*

Here's another angle: what if the main fantasy threat—say, a mind-binding magical crown—only attaches to those who feel unworthy of power? Suddenly, defeating the villain isn't just about winning a fight. It's about *believing* in your own value. The romance can support this. Maybe the love interest sees the protagonist's worth long before they do. Maybe loving someone else becomes the very reason they *finally* love themselves.

Again, the magic isn't just flashy—it's personal.

Ask yourself:

- What is my protagonist afraid of emotionally?
- What do they need to learn in order to love fully?
- What inner wound are they carrying that needs to be healed?

Now turn that into *something magical*. A creature. A realm. A prophecy. A task. A piece of magic that won't cooperate until the character grows. And the beauty is, you never have to say, "this magic represents grief" or "this curse equals shame." You just let it unfold. Let readers feel it. That's what great metaphor does.

You can even build your entire world around a central emotional theme. If your story is about *control versus surrender*, maybe the whole magic system is about learning to let go. Those who grip too tightly can't use it. If your theme is *connection versus isolation*, maybe the world is fractured into floating islands, and only love can build bridges.

Fantasy becomes the landscape of the soul.

And this works for side characters too. Maybe your rival character is tethered to a shadow creature that feeds on resentment. Maybe your protagonist's sibling can't speak unless someone speaks to them first, because they were raised in silence. These little metaphors aren't just neat—they're emotional shortcuts. They tell us who people are and what they carry, without spelling it out in monologue or exposition.

You can use ChatGPT to generate metaphors like this fast:

"Give me magical afflictions that reflect emotional wounds, like guilt, shame, or fear of intimacy."

"Suggest worldbuilding ideas where the land responds to love, trust, or grief."

"Create a fantasy curse that forces emotional growth before it can be broken."

The ideas don't have to be subtle right away. You can refine and adapt. The key is starting from the *emotional truth* and building outward into magic—not the other way around.

Sometimes, the metaphor shows up *after* you've written the scene. Maybe you wrote a moment where two characters cross a river together. If you look at it with fresh eyes, you might realize—oh. That was the moment they emotionally crossed a threshold, too. Now you can echo that river later. Use it symbolically. Maybe the river runs dry when their bond breaks. Maybe it floods during their final sacrifice.

Metaphors, once discovered, can be echoed again and again for deeper meaning.

The most powerful Romantasy stories often *feel* like dreams—not because they're vague, but because everything feels emotionally charged. The land aches. The air pulses. The spells have rules, but they also have moods. Readers might not always be able to explain *why* a scene hit so hard, but they'll feel the truth of it.

That's the power of metaphor.

You don't need to overthink it. Just trust that every time you tie magic to emotion, you're building something richer than just plot. You're letting readers experience emotional transformation *viscerally*, through their senses and imagination. You're letting love mean more than just love—it becomes healing. Growth. Rebirth.

The Villain as a Mirror of the Romantic Struggle

Every great Romantasy needs a worthy antagonist. Not just a big bad who wants power or chaos, but someone whose presence *tests the love story*. Someone who doesn't just create external conflict, but *echoes* the internal one. Because the best villains aren't just threats—they're reflections. They show your lovers what they could become if they made the wrong choices. Or worse, if they gave in to fear.

Think about it like this: your villain is a distorted version of your romantic arc. Maybe they once fell in love and lost it—so now they believe love is a weakness. Maybe they crave control because they were once powerless in a relationship. Maybe they're obsessed with destiny because they were denied a choice. The point isn't to make the villain secretly a romantic lead. It's to make them a symbol of what your protagonists are afraid to face.

That way, when your main couple fights the villain, they're not just swinging swords or flinging spells. They're confronting *parts of themselves*.

Let's look at a classic example. Say your protagonist is afraid of intimacy. They're drawn to someone, but terrified of being known. Meanwhile, the villain thrives in isolation. They've built an entire kingdom on fear and distance, convinced that caring is what gets you killed. Suddenly, the fight isn't just for survival—it's about *choosing connection over control*. The romance and the plot become two sides of the same emotional journey.

This doesn't mean the villain and the love interest need to be connected by blood or backstory. But it helps if they represent different possible futures. One is the path of healing. The other is the path of avoidance, bitterness, obsession, or emotional stasis.

Ask yourself:

- What does my villain *believe* about love?
- How did they get hurt—and how did they respond to that pain?
- What fear or flaw do they have in common with my protagonist?

That's the emotional core. And you can build your villain from there.

Say your love story is about trust. One character has never let anyone in; the other wears their heart on their sleeve. The villain? They used to trust someone—until it got them betrayed. Now they manipulate, charm, and control. They see love as a weapon. That creates a triangle of meaning. The protagonists have to ask: are we different from them, or are we just pretending?

Or maybe your love story is about self-worth. The villain sees themselves as unlovable—so they try to become irreplaceable through power, immortality, magical domination. It doesn't matter who loves them, because they don't love themselves. The protagonist has to face that mirror and *choose differently*.

You can use ChatGPT to flesh this out:

"Create a villain whose emotional wound mirrors a Romantasy protagonist's fear of abandonment."

"Write a backstory for a villain who believes love always leads to betrayal."

"Suggest ways a Romantasy villain might test the protagonist's belief in true love."

The most compelling villains *understand* love. They just fear it. Or twist it. Or weaponize it. Maybe the villain was once in love with someone the protagonist reminds them of. Maybe they still are. Maybe they offer the protagonist a way out—"Don't be a fool. Walk away before it ruins you like it ruined me." That moment of temptation is more powerful than a hundred lightning bolts.

Here's a technique: let the villain *say* something that the protagonist secretly believes—but doesn't want to admit. Something like:

"They'll never love you once they know who you are."

"People like us don't get happy endings."

"You think love makes you strong? Look at what it's already cost you."

Those are knives in the gut. And they stick.

The villain doesn't need to be a monster. They might even be *right*—in a twisted way. Maybe their love was taken from them. Maybe their heart was used against them. But instead of healing, they calcified. That's what makes them dangerous. And tragic. And unforgettable.

If you want to go further, tie the villain's *magic* to their emotional flaw. If they're obsessed with control, maybe they manipulate time. If they fear abandonment, maybe their power traps people in illusions of perfect love. If they crave immortality, maybe they drain life from others to stay young—desperate to be loved forever, even if no one really knows them.

Let your villain's power *reflect* their emotional scar.

Now contrast that with your romantic leads. The protagonist might struggle with vulnerability—but chooses to open up anyway. The love interest might fear loss—but stays anyway. Every decision they make becomes a quiet rebellion against the villain's worldview.

That creates emotional stakes that no battle scene can match.

Even better? Let the villain *force* the romance to grow. Maybe they kidnap one character, pushing the other to cross emotional and magical limits to get them back. Maybe they use truth-telling spells to reveal things your couple was trying to hide. Maybe they disguise themselves as one of the lovers, creating a betrayal that tests everything.

The villain becomes the *forge*. The heat that tempers the bond. And when they're finally defeated—not just by strength, but by a choice to love anyway—it feels earned.

Of course, not every Romantasy villain needs to have a tragic love story. Some are just power-hungry tyrants. But even then, the best ones believe *something*. Something dangerous. Something your protagonists have to reject—not with a speech, but with a life lived differently.

In the end, your villain is a distorted love story. A warning. A version of your protagonist who gave up on connection, or twisted it into something else.

And when your characters choose love anyway—not just as a feeling, but as an *action*—they're not just defeating evil.

They're defeating fear.

The Third Act Breakup: Why It Hurts and Why It Matters

You knew it was coming. The moment where everything falls apart. The kiss is just a memory, the promises feel like lies, and one of your leads walks away—or is left behind. In Romantasy, the third act breakup isn't just expected. It's *necessary*. Not because readers love pain (although, let's be honest, they kind of do), but because this is where the romance stops being about attraction and starts being about *transformation*.

It hurts because it *has* to. It matters because it *changes* them.

Let's be real: in the first two acts, your characters are dancing around each other. Flirting. Resisting. Drawing close. Learning about each other in the middle of quests, magic, curses, and political drama. Maybe they kiss. Maybe they fight. Maybe they save each other or betray each other. But the real question—always—is this: **will they choose each other when it's hard?**

The third act breakup is where that question gets tested. Not with soft smiles or longing looks, but with *consequences*.

Maybe one character lies. Maybe they hide something—like a prophecy, a secret identity, a love bond they didn't ask for. Maybe they made a deal with the villain behind the other's back. Or maybe they just failed. Failed to protect. Failed to say what mattered. Failed to show up when it counted.

The breakup doesn't have to be loud. Sometimes, it's worse when it's quiet. A whispered goodbye. A slammed door. A slow walk away while the other character stands in shock, unable to follow.

And that pain? It's where the *real romance* begins.

Because love isn't about things going right. It's about what your characters do when everything's gone wrong.

The third act breakup isn't there just to create drama. It serves a purpose—several, actually.

One: It creates emotional climax.

This is the *heartbreak point*. The moment the characters lose not just each other, but something *in themselves*. Faith. Hope. A belief in the possibility of love. For a while, it feels like it can't be fixed. And that emotional low point makes the eventual reunion—if there is one—hit *so much harder*.

Two: It forces character growth.

Your lovers have flaws. That's part of what makes them compelling. The breakup shows where those flaws collide. Maybe one character clings to control. The other needs honesty. The breakup forces them to confront the parts of themselves they've been avoiding. And when they come back together, it's not because the world got easier. It's because *they got stronger*.

Three: It gives love stakes.

If everything goes smoothly, the romance feels shallow. If they break up and still *choose* each other afterward, the romance feels earned. Sacrificed for. Battled for. Reclaimed.

But here's the key: don't just break them up for shock value. Break them up in a way that makes *emotional sense*. The best third act breakups feel inevitable. You want your readers screaming "No!" but also thinking, "Of course."

It should feel like a heartbreak that had been coming for chapters—one moment, one secret, one wound at a time.

Now let's talk mechanics. How do you write the actual breakup scene?

The best ones often combine two forces: **the personal wound** and **the external pressure**. Something inside them says, *I can't do this*. And something outside says, *You shouldn't*. Together, those forces make the breakup feel real. Maybe it's a choice between love and duty. Or love and power. Or love and survival.

A few examples:

- The protagonist finds out the love interest has been lying about their identity—and feels like the entire relationship is built on falsehood.
- The love interest sacrifices the protagonist's safety to save someone else—proving their heart lies elsewhere.
- A prophecy is revealed that says they can never be together without bringing doom to the world.
- One of them chooses revenge over forgiveness—and it tears the bond apart.

You can use ChatGPT to generate breakup scenarios like these:

"Give me five heartbreak moments in a Romantasy story where love and fate are at odds."

"Describe a magical misunderstanding that leads to a third act breakup between two bonded characters."

"Create a dramatic but emotionally believable breakup caused by a betrayal tied to a magical curse."

And don't forget the emotional fallout.

A good breakup scene doesn't end with the breakup. It echoes. It ripples through the next few chapters. Maybe one character can't sleep. Maybe the other throws themselves into danger, trying not to feel. Maybe they *almost* reach for each other again—and then don't.

Let your readers sit in that ache. It builds tension. It builds longing. It builds *hope*.

Because here's the thing: readers don't want perfection. They want *earned resolution*. So when your characters find their way back—when they apologize, or fight to win each other back, or sacrifice something to prove they've changed—it *matters*. That final kiss doesn't feel like a reward. It feels like *redemption*.

Of course, not every Romantasy has a happily ever after. Sometimes the third act breakup *is* the ending. And that's okay too—if it's honest. If it leaves the reader gutted, but understanding. Still, most readers come to Romantasy hoping for that reunion. That moment when love wins, not because it was easy, but because it was chosen.

Want to write an unforgettable breakup? Keep it simple. Raw. Specific.

Not:

"I don't love you anymore."

But:

"You looked me in the eye and lied—and the worst part is, I still wanted to believe you."

Or:

"You made me feel safe. And now I don't know if I'll ever feel safe again."

Oof. That's the stuff.

Break their hearts carefully. Truthfully. With emotional weight. Then let them earn their way back—not just to each other, but to *themselves*.

Writing Magical Action That Doesn't Break the Love Story

It's easy to get swept away by the spectacle. The battle scenes. The showdowns. The magical duels that shake the sky. Romantasy is part fantasy, after all—and with fantasy comes the thrill of action. But here's the danger: if you lean too hard into the magic and the mayhem, the *romance* can get lost. The love story that was simmering beneath the surface suddenly disappears beneath spellfire and swordplay.

So how do you write magical action *without* breaking the emotional spine of your Romantasy? How do you keep the romance *alive* even while everything is exploding around it?

You make sure the action doesn't just serve the plot—it serves the *relationship*.

Let's start with a core idea: every scene of magical action should either *complicate*, *test*, or *reveal* something about the romantic bond. If it's not doing one of those things, it might be better off as a page in someone else's fantasy novel.

For example, don't just have your characters fight side by side because it looks cool. Show us what fighting together *means* to them. Maybe one character is reckless in battle and the other is methodical. Maybe their strengths clash. Maybe one protects the other and it leads to a power struggle. Or maybe, just maybe, one of them hesitates in the middle of the fight—because they're afraid to lose the person they love.

Now *that* kind of action deepens the romance.

Think of the battlefield as a crucible. It burns away the small talk, the illusions, the distance. Under pressure, people show who they really are. Do they trust each other? Do they put the other first, even when it's dangerous? Do they make selfish choices—or selfless ones?

Here's a strong example: imagine a scene where the love interest goes into a magical fight alone, telling the protagonist to stay back. They don't want them to get hurt. But the protagonist disobeys—because love *isn't* safe, and they're not willing to watch from the sidelines. That act isn't just action. It's a *romantic turning point*.

Use ChatGPT to help plot moments like this:

"Give me magical combat scenes in a Romantasy where the fight tests the trust between lovers."

"Write a battle where one romantic lead uses magic to save the other—against their wishes."

"Describe an action scene that ends in a confession, not a victory."

Even better, build action scenes around *emotional beats*. Maybe your couple is fighting *each other*. Literally. One's been enchanted, or turned into a monster, or forced into betrayal. That's drama with teeth. Every swing, every spell, is laced with heartbreak.

Or go the other way—let action *bring them together*. Maybe there's a magical bond that only activates under pressure. Maybe they share a spell that requires perfect synchronization. Maybe they cast a spell together for the first time—and it works because their hearts are aligned.

That's not just good magic. That's good romance.

Also think about what's said—or not said—during action. A character screaming "Don't you dare die on me!" mid-fight is cliché, sure, but it's also effective. Even better? Silence. A shared look across a battlefield. A moment where everything slows down, and one character sees the other surrounded—and *chooses them* over the objective.

It's not about saying "I love you" with words. It's about saying it with *actions*—literally.

Another tip: make sure magic *costs* something. If spells come easy, or if no one ever bleeds, there's no tension. And without tension, romance has no friction. But if using magic *hurts*, if casting a spell leaves a scar or drains memory or risks the caster's soul? Now we're talking.

Now imagine this: a character sacrifices their magic to save the person they love. Not their life—their *freedom*. Their identity. Their power. That kind of moment stays with a reader forever.

Magic can also be intimate. Think of how two characters might link their magic in a physical way—by holding hands, or sharing breath, or touching foreheads. Think about rituals that require closeness. Spells that require emotional truth to work. You're not just writing a battle scene. You're writing a *love scene with fire and teeth*.

Of course, some action scenes will be broader. Big wars. Factions colliding. Cities falling. When that happens, keep anchoring us in the emotional center. What is *this couple's* stake in the chaos? Are they trying to protect each other? Rescue someone? Fulfill a prophecy that might pull them apart?

Even in a massive climax, the reader's heart is tethered to the romance. If we don't know what this fight *means* to the characters—individually and together—it just becomes noise.

Think about structure, too. Don't let action sequences go on so long they push out the character development. If your climax has a huge battle, break it up with smaller, personal moments. A conversation behind enemy lines. A kiss before a suicide mission. A realization that loving someone means letting them go into danger *anyway*.

You can also reverse things: use romance to *stop* the action. A character drops their weapon. Refuses to fight. Offers themselves in trade. Confesses love to break a curse. These moments are unforgettable precisely because they use romance to interrupt violence.

And if your couple fights *together*? Let that fight be choreographed like a dance. Complementary magic. Mirrored movements. A trust so complete, they don't need to speak. These scenes feel like poetry in motion—and when they're done right, they become the kind of thing readers reread five times in a row just to feel the beat of it again.

Finally, don't forget the aftermath. What do your characters say *after* the danger has passed? How do they treat each other when the blood's still drying and the world has shifted?

"I thought I lost you."

"You did. But I came back anyway."

"You shouldn't have."

"Don't care."

Those four lines say more than a love letter.

ChatGPT as a Brainstorming Machine for Pivotal Scenes

So you've built the world, created the characters, structured the plot, and added all the magic, metaphor, and heartbreak your Romantasy needs. But now you're staring down one of *those* moments. You know the kind—the pivotal scene. The first kiss. The brutal betrayal. The sacrifice. The reunion. The scene that's supposed to make your readers cry, cheer, gasp, or throw the book across the room and immediately pick it up again.

And suddenly... you're stuck.

This is where ChatGPT becomes less of a tool and more of a *creative partner*. When you're at the edge of a scene and you know it needs to hit hard, but you're not quite sure how to structure it, escalate it, or even start it—this is when you call in reinforcements. Not to write it for you. But to **light a fire under your imagination**.

The beauty of ChatGPT is that it doesn't run out of ideas. It's a brainstorm engine that doesn't need coffee breaks or reassurance. You can throw scene prompts at it all day and it will keep feeding you options until one *clicks*. And sometimes the idea that clicks isn't even one you use directly—it's the *third one down*, the thing it made you think of because something in the suggestion sparked a better version in your own voice.

Let's walk through how to use ChatGPT to crack pivotal scenes wide open.

Step One: Frame the emotional goal.

Every pivotal scene has an emotional spine. What's the *feeling* you want the reader to walk away with? Do you want them to feel devastation? Yearning? Catharsis? Surprise? The goal isn't to write the scene yet—it's to define the emotion you're chasing. Once you know that, you can ask for ideas that *aim at that feeling*.

Try this prompt:

"Give me five Romantasy scenes that end in emotional devastation without killing either character."

Or:

"What's a creative way for two characters to realize they're soulbound—without a big magical info-dump?"

You're asking for *scenarios*, not sentences. You want setups, angles, frameworks. Things that give you room to write your way in.

If you're stuck on a reunion scene, try:

"Write three reunion ideas for lovers who broke up over a betrayal—but still love each other."

Each one will have a different tone. One might be angsty. Another tender. A third furious. The variety is gold.

Step Two: Drill down into the moment.

Once you have the setup, use ChatGPT to explore *how* the scene could unfold.

Say you're writing a magical kiss that breaks a curse. You could ask:

"Describe three different ways a kiss could break a curse in a Romantasy setting—one tragic, one comedic, one surprising."

Or:

"Write dialogue for a Romantasy scene where the lovers kiss for the first time, knowing it might kill them both."

You don't have to use the words it gives you. What you're doing here is pressure-testing the idea. Seeing how it feels. Often, reading even a few sample lines helps you figure out the tone you want—or don't want.

Step Three: Mix emotional layers.

Pivotal scenes are rarely about *just* the plot. They're layered. You can ask ChatGPT to help you layer in emotion by stacking conflicting feelings.

Try:

"Give me ideas for a Romantasy scene where the protagonist saves the love interest—but is furious with them the entire time."

Or:

"Write a moment where two characters kiss in the middle of an argument—and the kiss makes everything worse."

These are the kinds of dynamics that make a scene *memorable*. Complex, charged, unbalanced in the best way.

And if you feel like your pivotal scene is missing tension, ask for reversals:

"Suggest twists that could happen *during* a confession scene in a Romantasy story."

"Give me ideas for a betrayal scene where the betrayed character doesn't realize it at first."

Adding uncertainty makes your turning points sharper.

Step Four: Map cause and effect.

Sometimes the hardest thing about a pivotal scene is not the moment itself—but *what leads to it*. If you need help building toward the scene, ask for a sequence of events.

For example:

"Outline three scenes that naturally build toward a Romantasy character confessing love they've hidden for years."

"What would need to happen before a Romantasy character sacrifices their magic for someone else?"

This gives you a breadcrumb trail. A way to walk toward the big moment with intention.

Step Five: Keep it personal.

Don't forget, ChatGPT gets better results the more *specific* you are. Instead of saying "give me a dramatic scene," say:

"I have a Romantasy story where a fire mage has fallen in love with a water spirit. They're on opposite sides of a magical war. Suggest three intense reunion scenes after their betrayal in the second act."

Now you're feeding the system actual stakes. You're not just asking for ideas—you're asking for *your* story's ideas.

And if you're halfway through a scene and it's not working? Paste it in and say:

"How can I raise the emotional stakes here?"

"What would make this moment more surprising or intimate?"

"Suggest a twist that would turn this almost-kiss into a moment of heartbreak."

ChatGPT becomes a collaborator who always has ideas, even if you're exhausted.

Bonus Tip: Use "What If" chains

One of the best ways to use ChatGPT is to keep following the "what if" thread.

Start with:

"What if the love interest is cursed to forget the protagonist every time they fall asleep?"

Then follow up:

"What if the protagonist *uses* that forgetting to keep the love interest safe?"

"What if the villain knows this and uses it against them?"

"What if the love interest starts remembering anyway—but pretends not to?"

Suddenly, you've built an entire emotional arc around a single idea. That's how you turn brainstorming into storytelling.

In the end, ChatGPT isn't here to write the whole scene for you—it's here to *unstick you*. To throw sparks at the page until one of them catches. To help you find the version of the scene that feels like *you*, only bolder.

And pivotal scenes are worth this kind of attention. They're the moments readers remember. The chapters they highlight. The scenes they quote in fan art, fanfic, and reviews.

Don't settle for "good enough" when it comes to your story's emotional backbone.

In the next chapter, we'll pull back the curtain on endings—how to wrap your Romantasy with heart, weight, and just the right touch of magic that lingers.

Let's write an ending that sings.

What Makes a Romantasy Ending Satisfying (Even If It's Bittersweet)

Every Romantasy has to end—but not all endings are created equal. Some tie everything up in a perfect bow. Some end with tears and wreckage. Some leave a little ache, a lingering note that hums in the chest long after the book is closed. Whether you're writing a happy ending or a bittersweet one, the goal isn't to deliver *exactly what the reader expects*. The goal is to give them something that feels *true*. Something that honors the journey they've taken. Something that makes them sigh—not because it's over, but because it *meant something*.

So what makes a Romantasy ending feel satisfying?

Let's start with this: it needs to feel *earned*.

That means your characters have grown. They've faced the internal fears and emotional obstacles that kept them from being together. They've made hard choices. They've hurt each other, healed, sacrificed, risked, changed. The ending doesn't have to be a wedding or a crown or a sunset kiss—but it does need to show that the story mattered. That everything they went through brought them *here*, to this final choice.

In Romantasy, where the stakes often include not just hearts but kingdoms, curses, and destiny itself, the ending should balance the personal and the epic. The fate of the world is cool—but what we *care* about most is whether they reach for each other, whether they still believe in love after everything.

Maybe your lovers survive, but they're changed. Maybe they don't get to stay together, but they *do* get to say goodbye. Maybe one becomes immortal and the other doesn't—and that hurts—but there's still peace, still tenderness, still a promise that echoes forward. These kinds of endings hurt in the best way.

That's the difference between sad and *bittersweet*. Sad says: this hurts and it's over. Bittersweet says: this hurts *because* it mattered. And sometimes, that's even more powerful than happily-ever-after.

Still, if you're aiming for a happy ending, that's absolutely valid—especially in Romantasy. The genre thrives on emotional payoff. But even happiness needs texture. If the couple comes together too easily at the end, it feels flat. If they've been torn apart, betrayed, broken, and still find their way back? Now we believe in the bond.

You can use ChatGPT to brainstorm emotionally layered resolutions:

"Give me Romantasy ending scenarios that are hopeful but not unrealistic."

"Suggest bittersweet Romantasy endings where the lovers part for good reasons but stay emotionally connected."

"Write a final scene where a broken magical bond is repaired—not by power, but by love."

These prompts help you think in terms of *feeling*, not just plot.

Let's talk structure for a second. The last chapter or scene of your book doesn't need to tie up *everything*. In fact, some of the best endings leave a few threads open—but only the right ones. Questions about love, character arcs, and theme should feel closed or resolved. Political futures, world-building tangents, or side character fates? Those can stay a little hazy if needed.

Readers don't need full closure on every detail. They need *emotional closure*. A sense that the arc has completed. That the version of the character we met in chapter one couldn't have made the choice they make in the final pages.

That's growth. That's satisfaction.

Now, if you're planning a series or a sequel, the balance gets trickier. You want to leave doors open—but still give readers a reason to feel like they've *finished* something. A romantic arc can close even if a political arc doesn't. A magical conflict can end even if a larger war looms. What you want is resolution that feels meaningful *now*, even if more story is coming later.

One of the most powerful tools for a Romantasy ending is **echo**. Bring something back. A line of dialogue. A symbol. A small gesture that now means something different. The scarf that was once a shield becomes a gift. The phrase that once felt like banter now lands like a promise. The place where they first fought becomes the place where they kiss again.

This kind of storytelling symmetry makes an ending feel *complete*. Like a circle closing.

Another trick? Let the ending reflect the **theme**. If your Romantasy was about trust, then the ending should show trust earned, tested, and chosen. If it was about identity, then let your character *claim* who they are. If it was about sacrifice, then the ending needs to *cost* something. That's what gives the romance weight.

Here's an example: say your protagonist is cursed to forget the person they love every time they fall asleep. At the end, they choose to break the curse by giving up all their memories—including the ones they've made. But the final line? The love interest smiling as the protagonist walks in, eyes lighting up like it's the first time *and* the last. That's bittersweet. That's full circle. That *hurts so good*.

Readers don't need every story to end in fireworks. But they do need to *feel*. Let them cry. Let them ache. Let them hope. And above all—let them believe that what happened *mattered*.

If you're not sure your ending hits emotionally, use ChatGPT to test it:

"What emotion does this ending create?"

"Suggest alternate endings that raise the emotional payoff."

"What could this final scene echo from earlier in the story to make it more satisfying?"

Sometimes all you need is one tweak. One callback. One line that turns a soft goodbye into a scar that readers *want* to carry.

In the end, a Romantasy ending should feel like the last note of a song. Maybe it's triumphant. Maybe it's sad. Maybe it's soft and strange and unexpected. But it lingers. It resonates. It reminds the reader that magic isn't just power—it's *emotion*. And love? Love is the most dangerous, transformative magic of all.

The Balance of Hope and Pain in the Final Chapter

The final chapter of your Romantasy isn't just where the plot winds down. It's where the heart of the story speaks one last time. And whether you're writing a sweeping happy ending, a devastating farewell, or something delicate and unresolved, there's one thread that binds all satisfying finales together: the balance of hope and pain.

Too much pain, and it feels hollow. Too much hope, and it can feel unearned. But get the balance right, and your reader will close the book with a deep breath—the kind that says, *that hurt, but it healed too.*

Romantasy, more than most genres, walks the line between light and dark. Magic comes with cost. Love comes with risk. The entire story often revolves around two people trying to love each other in a world determined to keep them apart. That's why endings that acknowledge *both* the wounds and the wonder feel the most authentic.

Let's talk about the **pain** first.

Pain is proof of the journey. It shows that your characters have struggled, lost, fought, and bled for what they have. It doesn't always have to be dramatic—someone doesn't need to die, the world doesn't have to end—but there should be a cost. Maybe it's something that's lost along the way: a home, a friend, a magical gift, a version of themselves they had to leave behind.

A satisfying final chapter doesn't ignore that cost. It leans into it. It lets the reader *feel* the aftermath. Even if the lovers reunite, even if peace is won, there's value in taking a quiet moment to acknowledge what it took to get there.

A character might be smiling while holding the person they love—but thinking about who didn't survive. Or how things will never be as they once were. That's not depressing. That's *human*. That's depth.

Pain also makes joy richer. If your couple has been through hell, then even the smallest moment of tenderness at the end—a touch, a smile, a look—feels *earned*. The reader remembers the near-loss, the breakup, the sacrifice. They don't need a grand speech. Sometimes the best line is:

"You stayed."

Now let's talk about **hope**.

Hope is why readers show up. No matter how dark or wild or heavy the story gets, most Romantasy readers want to believe that love can survive. That magic can heal. That no matter how broken someone feels, they can still be whole again.

Hope doesn't mean everything is perfect. It means *something is possible*. A future. A rebuilding. A sense that the worst is over and the next chapter—whatever it holds—will be faced together.

Even in bittersweet endings, there's room for this. Maybe the lovers part, but with peace. Maybe one of them has to walk away, but leaves behind a gift, a message, a symbol of love that endures. Maybe they don't get their forever—but they got *this moment*. And that was worth everything.

One of the strongest tools you can use in the final chapter is **echo**. Bring something back from earlier in the story—a line, a place, a symbol—and let it mean something new now. The scarf that once represented guilt now symbolizes freedom. The cave where they first argued becomes the place where they finally kiss. The nickname that once irritated is now said with a smile.

Echoes carry emotional weight. They make readers feel like the story *came full circle*.

You can use ChatGPT to brainstorm ending beats that strike this balance:

"Give me Romantasy final scenes that are both hopeful and emotionally raw."

"Suggest a last line that feels like closure but still hurts a little."

"Describe a Romantasy ending that uses a small, quiet gesture to show love survived."

Also think about **pacing**. The final chapter doesn't need to rush. In fact, this is often the moment to *slow down*. Let the reader sit with the aftermath. Let your characters breathe. Let us feel the quiet. If there's been war, let us see the sunrise. If there's been heartbreak, let us hear the words they were too afraid to say earlier. If they're going to part, let us feel every second of it. And if they're staying together? Let it be intimate. Not flashy. A shared meal. A moment of stillness. A plan for the future, however uncertain. Hope isn't loud. Hope is soft—and defiant.

One of the best ways to create this balance is to let your characters *change*. Let them show us, in that final chapter, who they've become. Maybe the emotionally closed-off protagonist finally says "I love you." Maybe the impulsive fighter waits. Maybe the protector lets themselves be protected.

Let them grow. Let the love story *change them*.

And don't be afraid to leave a little space. Not every ending needs a full epilogue. Sometimes the best final lines are the ones that leave the door cracked open.

"She looked up—and he was there, just like he promised."

"They stepped into the mist together, hand in hand, whatever came next."

"It wasn't over. Not yet. But it would be, one day—and that was enough."

These lines hold both pain and hope. They suggest there's more to come—even if the story ends here.

The final chapter is the emotional exhale. It's the slow fade, the last heartbeat, the echo of everything your characters endured. It should feel *true* to them. Not perfect. Not clean. But honest. Real. And it should leave your reader with the sense that even if they're crying, they're glad they came.

In the next chapter, we'll dive into how to edit your Romantasy—without sanding down its soul. Because writing the end is only part of the journey. Making it shine comes next.

Revising with Heart: Editing a Story That Sings

You wrote the story. You made it through the romance, the magic, the battles, the heartbreak, the healing. And now you're staring at the finished draft—your Romantasy. It's rough. It's raw. It's full of moments that work and others that wobble. Maybe there are scenes that feel too flat, too fast, or just plain weird. That's okay. Because now comes the part where the book finds its *voice*.

Revising isn't about making the story "correct." It's about making it *sing*. And to do that, you have to revise with *heart*.

Let's start here: editing is not just about fixing grammar or tightening dialogue. Those are steps—but they come later. First, you want to look at your story the way a reader would. Feel the rhythm. Find the emotion. Listen for the places where the story pulses—and the places where it goes quiet, but not in a good way.

The most important question to ask during revision isn't "Is this well-written?" It's "*Does this make me feel something?*"

That's your North Star.

Start with the **big beats**. Read through the whole manuscript (or let ChatGPT summarize it with you, if you want an overview). As you go, mark every moment that feels emotionally alive. The scenes where the characters break open. The lines that catch your breath. The kisses, the fights, the confessions. Then look for the scenes that feel... flat. Rushed. Over-explained. These are the places you'll want to dig into.

Ask yourself:

- Is this scene doing *emotional work*?
- Does it push the character or relationship forward?
- Does it *feel* like it belongs in this book?

If the answer is no, don't be afraid to cut it—or reshape it entirely.

Here's where ChatGPT becomes your secret weapon. Not to rewrite for you, but to *help you figure out what's missing*. Try prompts like:

"What would raise the emotional stakes in this confrontation scene?"

"How can I deepen the tension in this near-kiss without adding more plot?"

"This chapter feels flat—what kind of internal conflict could the character be facing here?"

It's like having a brainstorming partner who never gets tired.

Now, when it comes to the **romantic arc**, revision is everything. First drafts often underplay or overplay the emotional progression. Maybe they go from enemies to lovers too fast. Maybe the tension fizzles in the middle. Maybe the third-act breakup doesn't land.

Re-read the romance as if *that* is the only story. Trace every beat. Are the emotional turning points clear? Does the connection deepen with each encounter? Do they have moments of vulnerability, friction, and choice?

Use ChatGPT to map it:

"List the major emotional beats in this romantic arc."

"Suggest a moment of conflict that would feel natural between these two characters after this kiss scene."

"What kind of gesture could show forgiveness without needing a big speech?"

Next, revise your **magic** and **worldbuilding** in service of character. This is Romantasy, after all—not a lore manual. If the worldbuilding overwhelms the emotion, scale it back. If the magic isn't doing anything *personal*, sharpen it until it does. The most effective fantasy elements reflect what your characters are feeling, fearing, or fighting for.

For example, instead of long passages explaining the rules of time-travel spells, focus on what it *means* for a character to cast one knowing it might erase a memory—or a moment of love. That's magic that sings.

During revision, look for opportunities to use **symbolism**. Is there an image or motif that can echo across the story? A song, a star, a piece of jewelry, a repeated phrase? These touches become anchors. Emotional shorthand. They remind readers that the story is more than plot—it's *poetry*.

And here's the part most writers forget: revise your **quiet moments**, too.

Romantasy thrives on intensity, yes—but it breathes in the silence. The campfire conversations. The glances across a room. The stillness after a spell ends. These are the spaces where love blooms. Make sure you're not rushing past them in the pursuit of plot. Slow down. Let your characters sit in their own feelings.

Use ChatGPT to shape those moments if needed:

"Give me internal monologue options for a character sitting beside someone they love but can't touch."

"What might a character notice while watching their love interest sleep after a fight?"

"Describe a quiet post-battle scene where two lovers reconnect without saying much."

When you revise with heart, you're not just editing words. You're tuning emotion. You're turning your book into something that *feels alive*. As you polish your prose, make sure you're not sanding down the *spark*. Not everything needs to be perfectly structured. Not every line needs to be clever. But every beat should ring *true*.

Read your dialogue out loud. Feel the rhythm of the sentences. If something clunks, change it. If it sings, keep it—even if it breaks some imaginary rule.

This is your story. Your voice. Make it sound like *you*—just sharper, braver, more emotionally precise.

And yes, you'll probably go through more than one revision. That's part of the process. Each round is another chance to peel back the surface and find the soul. Don't be afraid to kill your darlings—but don't be afraid to *rescue* them either. Sometimes a scene that doesn't work in chapter four *belongs* in chapter twenty. Sometimes the line you almost deleted becomes the final sentence.

Trust your instincts. Follow the feeling.

When you're done, your book may not be perfect. But it will be yours. Full of ache and magic and heart. It will carry the scars of revision like armor. It will speak to your readers in the language only stories know.

Asking ChatGPT for Line-Level Edits with Emotional Weight

You've revised the big scenes, trimmed the fat, filled the gaps, and layered your Romantasy with heart, heat, and magic. The structure feels right. The character arcs land. The romance pulses. Now you're standing at the finish line of the creative marathon, looking down at the line-level details—the individual words, sentences, beats, and turns of phrase that make your story shine.

This is where you ask: *Does this line not just say something—but make you feel something?*

And this is also where ChatGPT becomes your secret editor. Not the kind that tells you you've used too many adverbs (although it can), but the kind that listens for *emotional tone*. The one that helps you say things in a way that hits deeper. Harder. Truer.

Let's be clear: line-level editing is about more than "sounding pretty." It's about *emotional precision*. It's about making every sentence carry weight. Every bit of dialogue feel real. Every kiss feel inevitable. Every heartbreak feel earned.

And when you need help? That's where your writing partner with infinite patience—ChatGPT—steps in.

Step One: Start with Intention

Before you throw a paragraph at ChatGPT and ask, "Can you make this better?", ask yourself: *What do I want the reader to feel here?* That's the target. Whether it's tension, desire, betrayal, or quiet grief, your line edits should pull toward that emotional truth.

Instead of saying:

"Make this sound cooler,"

Try:

"Rewrite this paragraph to reflect quiet desperation without being melodramatic."

Or:

"Can you add more emotional weight to this line? It's the moment she realizes he's not coming back."

The more specific you are about your emotional goal, the more useful the response will be.

Step Two: Focus on High-Impact Moments

There's no need to polish every single line. Focus on the ones that matter most—confessions, rejections, turning points, discoveries, and quiet emotional beats that could use more resonance.

Try something like this:

Original: "He touched her arm, and she flinched."

Prompt: "Rewrite this moment to show that the touch reminds her of a memory she's tried to bury."

ChatGPT might give you:

"His fingers brushed her arm, and her breath caught—not from the contact, but from the ghost of a memory it dragged up, sharp and sudden as a knife in silk."

See the difference? Same beat. More *feeling*.

Step Three: Test Alternatives

Line edits are all about finding the *best* way to say something. And sometimes, that means testing three or four variations before something clicks.

You can ask:

"Give me three different versions of this line that emphasize emotional restraint."

"Write this internal monologue as if she's trying not to cry but can't stop the thoughts."

"Can you rewrite this short paragraph in a more lyrical, romantic style?"

Now you're not just fixing words—you're *finding tone*. One version might be too flowery. Another too blunt. The third? Just right.

Step Four: Sharpen Dialogue

Dialogue is one of the easiest places to lose emotional clarity. A love confession can sound cliché. A fight can fall flat. A goodbye might lack bite.

Paste the scene and ask:

"Can you rewrite this argument so both characters sound more hurt than angry?"

"Make this love confession feel like it's being said for the first time, with fear and hope."

"She's trying to say goodbye without admitting how much it hurts. Can you help soften the words while making the pain clear?"

ChatGPT doesn't just make it cleaner—it makes it *deeper*.

You can even play with voice:

"Rewrite this line in a more poetic tone, without losing clarity."

"Make this sound like something he's repeating to himself to keep from falling apart."

"How would this sound if she's trying to be brave, but her voice keeps cracking?"

You'll be amazed how just a few word changes can shift the emotional temperature of a scene.

Step Five: Keep the Original Voice

One concern many writers have when editing with ChatGPT is losing their own style. Here's the trick: don't accept a rewritten sentence just because it sounds "better." Accept it if it sounds *truer*. If it fits your tone, your world, your characters.

Use ChatGPT's suggestions as *scaffolding*. Start with its phrasing, then adjust. Soften it. Sharpen it. Replace a word. Flip the sentence. Let it guide you toward something you would've said—but hadn't quite found yet.

Think of it as a mirror that reflects your line back with more light.

And if the suggestion feels too generic, push harder:

"That's too vague. Make it more specific to their relationship—she's scared to love someone again."

"It sounds too formal. She's sarcastic and angry. Try again with more bite."

"Make it feel like he's choking on the words, not rehearsing them."

ChatGPT listens. And it adapts.

Step Six: Ask for Rhythm and Flow

Sometimes your writing needs music, not just meaning. Ask for help with flow:

"Smooth out this paragraph while keeping the emotional tone intact."

"Rewrite this monologue to build tension, like it's spiralling toward a confession."

"Can you adjust the rhythm of this sentence so it reads like a breathless thought?"

The difference between a good line and a *great* one often comes down to rhythm. Don't be afraid to fine-tune until it feels *just right*.

Step Seven: Let Yourself Feel It Again

The last step in line-level editing is *feeling*. Read the revised lines out loud. Sit with them. If they give you chills—or make your chest tighten—you've done it. That's the magic.

If they don't? Keep pushing.

You're not just polishing. You're sculpting moments that linger. That sting. That soothe. That *sing*.

In the final moments of your Romantasy, you're tuning your story like a stringed instrument. Every word is a note. Every pause is breath. You're not editing for perfection. You're editing for *resonance*.

And with ChatGPT at your side, you never have to stare at a flat sentence again and wonder, "How do I say this better?" You can ask. You can explore. You can iterate until the words stop sounding like lines—and start sounding like *feeling*.

Congratulations. You didn't just write a story.

You brought it to life.

Using Prompts to Deepen Emotional Arcs

When you strip a Romantasy story down to its bones, what holds it all together isn't the dragons, the magic, or the steamy kisses in enchanted forests. It's the emotional arc. The slow, painful, beautiful transformation of a character from someone who *can't* love to someone who *chooses* to love anyway. From someone who hides behind magic to someone who faces the truth. From someone who's afraid to be known to someone who says, "Here I am—take me as I am."

That's what readers come for. And that's what you're here to build.

But emotional arcs don't just happen because you write a few sad scenes and a couple of romantic gestures. They grow out of intention. They require careful thought, reflection, and shaping. And when you feel stuck or unsure where that emotional journey is headed—or how to push it deeper—this is where ChatGPT becomes your most valuable partner.

You're not just asking for plot ideas now. You're asking for *emotional evolution.*

You're looking to understand your characters not just as tools in a story, but as people who feel things deeply, who struggle, who grow—and who reflect the kind of emotional journey your readers are craving. And that's exactly what the right prompts can unlock.

Let's start with the **core of the emotional arc**. Think of it this way: what is your character *afraid of,* and what do they need to *learn* in order to be truly open to love?

You can ask:

"Help me identify my Romantasy protagonist's emotional wound and how it might affect their ability to fall in love."

"What might a character who was betrayed in the past believe about love, and how could that belief slowly unravel?"

"Give me emotional transformations for a Romantasy character who thinks vulnerability is weakness."

These kinds of prompts help you uncover the psychological blocks that drive your character's choices, conflicts, and resistance to love. Once you know that, you can design moments—plot points, dialogue, internal monologues—that *test* those beliefs.

It's not just about making them fall in love. It's about making them *change* in order to *become someone capable of love.*

Now let's zoom in to the **scenes that shape emotional arcs**. These are the turning points: when something cracks open, when a truth comes out, when a kiss doesn't land the way it was supposed to, when a sacrifice hurts more than expected.

Ask ChatGPT:

"Write three versions of a scene where a Romantasy character almost says 'I love you' but pulls back out of fear."

"Describe a moment where a character realizes their love interest is willing to walk away—and it terrifies them."

"What kind of small, quiet gesture could show emotional growth without needing dialogue?"

These scenes don't need to be big. In fact, some of the strongest emotional beats are *silent.* A hand reaching out and then pulling back. A letter never sent. A shield dropped mid-battle. A spell cast not to protect the world—but to protect one person.

If you're unsure *where* your characters are on their emotional arc, use prompts to help track their progress.

Try:

"List five key emotional beats that show a Romantasy protagonist learning to trust again."

"What are three scenes where my protagonist's fear of loss causes them to make the wrong choice?"

"Describe how a Romantasy love interest might slowly help someone with abandonment issues feel safe."

What you're doing here is building *emotional scaffolding*. You're making sure the heart of the story rises alongside the magic, the tension, and the romantic pull.

You can even use prompts to find *contrasts* in emotional arcs. Maybe one character believes in love from the start—but the other doesn't. That creates friction. Ask:

"How can two Romantasy characters with opposite views on love push each other to grow emotionally?"

"Give me conflict ideas between a character who wants freedom and one who wants commitment."

"Write a dialogue scene where both characters are right—but emotionally incompatible in that moment."

Conflict isn't just swords and curses. It's hesitation. Mismatched values. The fear of losing yourself in someone else. And when you explore that through prompts, you uncover ways to write scenes that are about *more* than what's happening on the surface.

One of the most powerful uses of prompts in this stage is to deepen *internal monologue*. That's where so much of the emotional weight lives—what the character *thinks*, but doesn't say. The stuff they bury. The things they wish they could take back.

Try this:

"Write an internal monologue for a Romantasy protagonist who's watching their love interest laugh with someone else—and trying to pretend it doesn't hurt."

"Give me thoughts for a character who realizes they've fallen in love—but can't say it because they're cursed."

"Describe the emotions of a character who's finally safe, but grieving everything it took to get there."

This is the language that wraps around your readers' hearts. It's how they see themselves in your character. And when it lands, it doesn't matter if the scene has firestorms and sword fights or just two people standing in a field under a grey sky—it will still *hurt* in the best way.

If you're feeling bold, go even deeper. Ask ChatGPT to *challenge* your character:

"What's the worst thing I could make this Romantasy protagonist face emotionally, and how might it change them?"

"Suggest a moment that forces the character to confront the fact that they're afraid of being loved."

"Write a scene where the character must choose between revenge and forgiveness—because the person they love is asking them to."

These aren't just plot points. They're the soul of your story.

Because in the end, Romantasy isn't just about the magic or the setting or the heat between characters. It's about *emotional transformation*. It's about building someone who begins the book broken in a specific way—and ends it not fixed, but *braver*. More open. Willing to try again.

Prompts don't replace your voice. But they give you the tools to sharpen it. They help you see through the fog of "what happens next" and into the emotional truth that makes it all *matter*.

So when you revise, or draft, or even daydream, start asking better questions. Get curious. Get personal. Ask about the fear. The lie. The wound. The belief that needs to be broken and rebuilt. Let ChatGPT help you name it, explore it, push it further than you thought you could.

And when your characters come out the other side changed—raw, but stronger—you'll know.

You didn't just write a love story.

You wrote an *emotional journey that lives in people's bones*.

Voice, Tone, and Style: Making It All Yours

You can write the most intricate magic system, plot the most heart-wrenching romance, and build emotional arcs that make people cry into their pillows—but if your story doesn't *sound* like you, something will always feel off. This is where **voice**, **tone**, and **style** come in. These are the invisible threads that hold the entire tapestry together. They're what make your Romantasy *yours*.

And the wild part? Most writers don't fully know what their voice is until they've written a lot—and edited even more. The good news? You don't need to have it figured out from page one. You just need to *listen for it*, nurture it, and—when needed—ask for a little help sharpening it.

So, let's break it down.

Voice: Who's Telling the Story?

Voice is the soul of the narration. It's the personality that speaks to your reader from the page. It might be lush and lyrical, sarcastic and sharp, dreamy and distant, earthy and raw. But it always *feels* like someone is telling you the story—someone specific, someone with a worldview, a rhythm, a cadence.

In Romantasy, your voice needs to carry both magic and emotion. It needs to hold space for wonder and heartbreak, tension and softness, beauty and danger. That doesn't mean it has to be flowery. Some of the strongest Romantasy voices are *quietly fierce* or *emotionally blunt*. What matters is consistency and authenticity.

Ask yourself:

- Does your narrator feel close to the character's emotional truth?
- Do the sentences feel like *them*—or like you trying to sound like someone else?
- Can you take a single paragraph out of your story and have someone say, "That sounds like you wrote it"?

That's voice.

Tone: How Does the Story *Feel*?

Tone is the emotional undercurrent of your scenes. It changes depending on what's happening. The tone of a breakup scene isn't the same as the tone of a reunion. The tone of a discovery scene isn't the same as a kiss.

Tone is what helps your reader know how to feel. It's the lighting, the soundtrack, the atmosphere—but built with words.

You control tone through sentence length, punctuation, vocabulary, and rhythm.

Short, clipped sentences? That's tension. Long, winding ones with soft consonants? That's probably tenderness or longing. Repetition can create obsession or spiraling grief. White space—those tiny one-line paragraphs—can create intimacy. Or dread.

The magic is in *how* you say what you're saying.

Use ChatGPT to test tone:

"Rewrite this paragraph to feel more wistful."

"Adjust the tone of this conversation to make it feel flirtatious but guarded."

"Make this battle scene feel less heroic and more desperate."

What you're doing is tuning the emotion without rewriting the whole idea. Think of it like color-grading a film.

Style: How Do You Build Your Sentences?

Style is the texture of your writing. It's your word choices, sentence structures, pacing, how you handle imagery, and how you use grammar (or break it). Style is where your fingerprints are most visible. It's not what you say. It's *how* you say it.

And style can evolve. You might write in a looser, more modern style for one story and something more poetic or baroque for another. That's okay. But it still needs to feel *intentional.*

If your story shifts tone or voice too abruptly between scenes—going from witty and casual to suddenly Shakespearean—it can jar the reader out of the experience. That doesn't mean you can't mix styles, but the shifts should feel earned and smooth.

Try this with ChatGPT:

"Rewrite this scene in a more lyrical style without losing clarity."

"Make this monologue sound more modern and emotionally vulnerable."

"Can you suggest synonyms that feel more in line with a dark Romantasy tone?"

And if you're not sure what your style is, ask ChatGPT to analyze it:

"Based on this excerpt, how would you describe my writing style?"

"What are three ways I can strengthen my stylistic voice in this Romantasy story?"

"Which parts of this passage feel consistent with a Romantasy tone, and which don't?"

Let your style grow from your characters, your world, and your themes. A story about wild fae magic might want a chaotic, vivid style. A story about forbidden love between rival spellcasters might benefit from restraint and understatement. A story about memory, grief, and devotion might need long, thoughtful prose that leaves space for silence.

There is no "right" style. But there is *your* style.

Don't Imitate. Adapt.

It's natural to read Romantasy you love and want to sound like those authors. Whether it's Laini Taylor, Sarah J. Maas, Holly Black, Naomi Novik, or someone indie you found in a fanfic spiral at 2am, those voices stick with you.

Let them *influence* you. But don't let them take over.

Instead, when you find a line or scene you love, ask:

- Why does this work?
- Is it the metaphor? The sentence rhythm? The emotional vulnerability?

Then apply that principle—not that sentence—to *your* story.

You can even run it through ChatGPT:

"This paragraph by [Author Name] really moves me. Can you explain why it works emotionally, and how I can use that effect in my own voice?"

You'll learn so much faster by breaking down what moves you—and then learning how to recreate it in your own way.

Voice in Dialogue

Let's not forget: your characters *also* have voices. Each one should speak with different rhythm, diction, and tone. That doesn't mean every character needs an accent or a catchphrase, but their dialogue should reflect their personality and past.

Ask ChatGPT:

"This character is guarded but clever. Can you help adjust their dialogue to reflect that?"

"Make this love interest sound a little more emotionally repressed but trying."

"Can you rewrite this romantic exchange so it sounds like two people who've known each other forever, not just met?"

When your character voices are distinct, your world feels lived in. Your romance feels *personal.*

Practice, Listen, Refine

Your voice is a living thing. It will shift over time, from story to story, even chapter to chapter. Don't stress about finding it immediately. Just *listen for it* as you go. When something feels like it hums—when a scene feels easy to write and emotional to read—that's a sign you're in your natural rhythm. And when something feels flat, generic, or forced? That's a flag to revisit tone, voice, or style.

This is where ChatGPT shines. Not in giving you the final answer, but in giving you *five different ways to hear the same moment*. One of them will sound more like you than the rest. That's your path forward.

Writing in First Person, Third Person, or Dual POVs

One of the first—and most powerful—choices you make in your Romantasy story is *point of view*. Not just who's telling the story, but *how* they're telling it. First person? Third person? Or something in between—maybe even dual points of view? This decision shapes your entire narrative voice, the emotional intimacy between reader and character, and the way your world feels as it unfolds.

It's not about what's right or wrong. It's about *what feels right for your story*.

Let's talk about your three main options—and how to use each of them to their fullest in Romantasy.

First Person: "I" Am the Story

First person is all about emotional immediacy. You're inside one character's head, heart, and skin. Everything that happens is filtered through their thoughts, their judgments, their emotions—raw, unfiltered, and incredibly personal.

This is a favorite for Romantasy because it makes the reader *feel* everything alongside the protagonist. Their first glimpse of the love interest? We feel it. Their magical trauma? We carry it. Their moment of transformation? It hits like it's our own.

When you write in first person, your job is to stay true to the character's perspective. They don't see the whole picture. They misread people. They can be blinded by emotion. But that's what makes it powerful.

First person also allows for a lot of interiority. You can fill the page with inner conflict, desire, fear, longing, hope, and confusion—and it feels natural. That's gold for Romantasy, where the characters often wrestle with both epic stakes and personal ones.

You can use ChatGPT to strengthen a first-person POV like this:

"Rewrite this paragraph to feel like an emotionally guarded character is forcing herself to admit she's falling in love."

"Give me internal thoughts for a Romantasy heroine who's trying not to cry after walking away from her soulmate."

First person is fantastic for unreliable narrators, slow-burn relationships, emotionally complicated arcs, and protagonists who are falling apart inside but trying to hold it together.

The trade-off? You're limited to one voice, one lens, one experience. If you want to show what another character is thinking or feeling—you can't. At least not directly.

Which brings us to...

Third Person: "She" Is the Story

Third person can be deep or distant, intimate or broad. It can feel as close as a whisper in the character's ear or as wide as a god watching from above. In Romantasy, third person is often used in what's called "deep third"—where you stay close to one character's internal perspective, but still use third-person grammar and structure.

Think of it like this: you're not *being* the character (like first person), but you're *riding in their skin*. You see what they see, feel what they feel—but you also get a little more flexibility in your phrasing, pacing, and transitions.

Third person can be great for Romantasy when you want to:

- Describe the world and magic with slightly more narrative distance.
- Keep the reader emotionally engaged but not fully trapped inside one head.
- Build suspense by showing action and reaction more fluidly.

Some writers find that third person gives them more control over *tone* and *style*. It lets you be lyrical without sounding too self-indulgent. It also gives you more freedom to switch between moments of intimacy and epic scope.

With ChatGPT, try prompts like:

"Rewrite this third-person paragraph to reflect quiet heartbreak without being dramatic."

"Adjust the narrative tone to feel more magical and romantic while staying close to the protagonist's emotions."

If your story has a large cast, complex politics, or magical systems that require explanation, third person can help you juggle it all while still keeping the reader emotionally grounded.

But what if you want *both* emotional intensity *and* multiple perspectives?

That's where dual POV comes in.

Dual POV: "I" and "He"—or "She" and "She"—Together

Dual POV means two (or sometimes more) characters tell the story. Often, this is the romantic pairing. You switch between their perspectives—sometimes by chapter, sometimes more flexibly. This is especially useful when your story hinges on *miscommunication*, secrets, conflicting goals, or parallel emotional journeys.

One of the best parts of dual POV is that it lets the reader *feel the tension from both sides*. You can show the moment one character realizes they're in love—and the other has no idea. Or one character is planning to leave while the other is planning to propose. That's the kind of emotional *dramatic irony* that Romantasy thrives on.

It also makes the romance feel more balanced. Both sides get a voice. Both sides get an arc.

But dual POV comes with challenges. You have to make sure each voice is distinct. If both characters sound the same, the reader can get confused or disengaged. It takes more work—but when it works, it's electric.

Try these prompts with ChatGPT to separate voices:

"Rewrite this passage in the love interest's voice—he's emotionally reserved, logical, and rarely says what he feels."

"Give me a first-person paragraph from the heroine's POV, and then the same scene from her love interest's POV with a different emotional read."

"How would these two characters describe the same kiss differently, based on their personalities and fears?"

You can also use dual POV to explore *contrasting relationships with magic*. Maybe one character sees magic as sacred, and the other sees it as dangerous. Maybe one trusts easily, and the other doesn't trust anyone at all. Their inner monologues will carry different weights—and show the reader how love builds bridges between different kinds of pain.

Some Romantasy authors write dual POV in first person ("I" from each character), others mix one first and one third, and some keep both in third. There's no rule. It's about what feels right—and what lets the emotional current of the story flow cleanest.

So... Which One Should You Choose?

Here's the secret: it's not about choosing the *best* POV. It's about choosing the one that makes your story feel *alive*.

Ask yourself:

- Whose emotions are the most important in this story?
- Do I want the reader to *be inside* the character—or close, but not submerged?
- Is this a love story about one person's transformation—or a mutual one?
- Does the story feel bigger than one mind can carry?

Try writing the same short scene in first and third person. Or from both characters' POVs. You'll feel it—the one that sparks, that sings, that feels easier to write because it just *fits*.

And if you change your mind halfway through? That's okay. It's your story. Let it tell you how it wants to be told.

Shaping Your World around the Central Romance

In Romantasy, the world isn't just a backdrop. It breathes. It pulses. It aches. And when done right, it doesn't just *host* the love story—it *mirrors* it, shapes it, and complicates it. The magic systems, kingdoms, mythologies, curses, and even landscapes should somehow reflect what your central couple is going through. The world should be another character in the relationship—a silent force that blesses, tests, or even threatens their bond.

When you shape your world around the central romance, you're making the setting *emotionally relevant*. That means the world isn't just about plot, lore, or rules. It's about *feeling*. It's about building a world that knows what love costs.

Let's start with the big question: What's the emotional core of your romance?

Is it about forbidden love? Second chances? Trust and betrayal? Power imbalance? Emotional healing? Once you know that, you can ask: *How can this world reflect, amplify, or challenge that emotional journey?*

For example, let's say your story is about a character who can't let anyone close because of a magical curse that causes harm when touched. That's not just a cool power. That's a world-built obstacle to intimacy. Suddenly, every moment of physical closeness is loaded with tension, longing, and fear. The world—and its magic—becomes a *metaphor* for the character's emotional walls.

Or maybe your characters are from warring nations where love between them is taboo. In that case, every rule, every symbol of loyalty, every custom and law becomes another wall between them. Even a shared meal might be scandalous. A glance across a battlefield might say more than a thousand words.

The world *tightens the screws* on the romance—and that's what makes readers care.

When building your world, start by asking ChatGPT things like:

"Give me ideas for magical laws or customs that would make falling in love dangerous."

"Suggest fantasy worlds where love is a source of power—and that power is feared."

"How could a fantasy society punish or prevent cross-class or cross-species relationships?"

The world you build should challenge your characters—but also offer chances to connect. If everything is against them, and there's never a moment of grace or beauty, the romance will suffocate. So build in safe places. Secret gardens. Forgotten temples. Night markets where no one asks questions. Magical bonds that only activate when the characters truly trust one another. Spaces where love *can breathe*, even if only for a moment.

Let's not forget how **settings** shape emotional tone. A Romantasy set in a crumbling palace steeped in shadows will have a different energy than one set in floating cities built from song. The setting whispers what kind of romance this is. Is it lush and sensual? Harsh and gritty? Soft and aching?

Even nature can echo emotional beats. A kiss under falling ash. A final goodbye in the middle of a blooming storm. The world should *feel* what the characters feel.

Ask ChatGPT:

"Describe a Romantasy setting where the world is healing as the characters heal."

"Give me a location where two characters could meet in secret—and where every detail heightens romantic tension."

"Suggest symbolic weather or natural phenomena that reflect emotional shifts in a love story."

You'll start to see how world and romance fold into each other like wind and flame.

Let's also talk **magic systems**. A great way to integrate world and romance is to give your magic emotional consequences. Think soulbonding, truth spells, curses tied to heartbreak, memory-sharing rituals, illusions that only break when someone's feelings are real.

Magic in Romantasy shouldn't just solve problems—it should *create them*, *complicate them*, and *reveal feelings your characters would rather keep buried*. Imagine a spell that shows your true emotions in glowing script across your skin. Imagine a prophecy that says one must die for the other to live. Imagine magic that lets you see someone else's dreams, and realizing they're dreaming of you.

Suddenly, your magic system *is* the romance.

Ask:

"What kind of Romantasy magic could force two characters to confront their feelings?"

"Suggest magical rituals that involve vulnerability or emotional sacrifice."

"Give me ideas for how a magical curse might parallel one character's fear of abandonment."

These prompts help you shape not just a functioning fantasy world, but an emotionally *relevant* one.

And don't forget **society**. The rules, expectations, and values of your world should influence how love is perceived. Maybe the society your characters live in doesn't value romantic love at all. Maybe arranged pairings are political, and anything based on emotion is considered weakness. Maybe love between certain races, magical orders, or bloodlines is forbidden—or required.

Ask ChatGPT to help you shape this:

"Describe a fantasy society where falling in love causes social shame or exile."

"What kinds of class systems or power structures might affect who someone is allowed to love?"

"Suggest cultural beliefs about soulmates in a Romantasy world."

When love goes against culture, it becomes an act of rebellion. And rebellion is *hot*—especially in a Romantasy.

But maybe your world is more nurturing. Maybe the society *believes* in soulmates. Maybe there's a tradition of leaving a carved stone at the door of the one you love, and that tradition is slowly fading—but your protagonist revives it. Maybe your world says that love is magic, and magic without love is empty.

Suddenly, even the lore supports your theme.

Here's the key takeaway: your world should *matter* to the romance. If you could move your characters into another fantasy setting and nothing changes emotionally, something's off. The world should *complicate*, *illuminate*, and *echo* the relationship.

So the next time you build a kingdom, forge a prophecy, or design a magical curse—ask yourself: *What does this mean for the love story?*

Because when your world and romance are woven tightly together, your story will feel bigger and more intimate all at once. Readers won't just remember the kiss or the betrayal. They'll remember the shadowed forest where it happened. The rules that said it was forbidden. The magic that made it possible—or impossible.

And most of all, they'll remember how your characters *fought* for love in a world that kept asking them not to.

Turning a Short Story into a Novel (or Vice Versa)

Romantasy stories come in all shapes and sizes. Sometimes the magic and love arrive in a tight burst of beauty—a single enchanted night, a stolen moment between curses. Other times, they stretch across kingdoms and generations. But what if your story lives somewhere in between? What if you've written a short story that feels like it wants to grow? Or maybe you've written a novel that feels bloated, and you're wondering if it actually wants to be something smaller, sharper, more focused?

Good news: you're not stuck. Stories are more flexible than they seem. With the right mindset and tools—including ChatGPT—you can scale a Romantasy story up or down and make it work in any format. It's not about padding or trimming. It's about *reshaping the emotional core* to fit the space you've got.

Let's start with **expanding a short story into a novel**.

The key question is: *What more do you want the reader to feel?* That's your path forward. A short story often captures a single emotional arc—like a forbidden kiss, a magical farewell, a reluctant alliance. If you want to turn that into a novel, ask what came *before* and what might come *after*.

Use ChatGPT like this:

"Help me expand this Romantasy short story into a novel by outlining a full character arc for the protagonist."

"What additional conflicts could arise if the lovers had to travel through enemy territory together?"

"Suggest subplots that could deepen the themes of love, fear, and sacrifice."

You're not just adding content—you're deepening resonance. Think about character backstories. Hidden truths. Side characters who weren't relevant in the short version but now deserve their own arcs. Settings that were once simple now become rich with lore.

Most importantly, stretch the **emotional journey**. If they fell in love in one scene in the short version, ask: what if that love had to be *earned* over time? What if it took ten near-misses, two betrayals, and one act of redemption?

Also consider worldbuilding. In a short story, you only have time to hint. In a novel, you can *show*. Maybe your characters are soulbound, but the magic is dying. Maybe your lovers are from opposite factions and have to fake a truce. Let the fantasy elements evolve alongside the romance.

You can ask ChatGPT to help layer this out:

"What's a slow-burn romance structure that can evolve across 30 chapters?"

"How could I introduce a prophecy or magical system that parallels the love story?"

"Give me ways to reveal backstory over time instead of in exposition dumps."

This turns your short spark into a full fire. Just don't forget: the novel version needs *movement*. New stakes. A midpoint crisis. A third-act break. It has to *go somewhere* emotionally and narratively, not just echo the short story again and again.

Now, let's look at the flip side: **trimming a novel down to a short story**.

This is about focus. What is the one emotional moment, the one magical truth, the one *relationship beat* that defines the entire arc?

If you could only keep one scene from the novel—what would it be?

That's your core.

Let's say your novel has a full enemies-to-lovers arc, with multiple battles and betrayals. To make it a short story, you strip away everything except one *intense encounter*. Maybe they're forced to work together to escape a crumbling temple. Maybe they've just fought and now have to hide in silence, side by side. Maybe it's the moment they part ways—without ever saying what they feel.

Ask ChatGPT:

"Help me compress this Romantasy novel into a short story centered on the final farewell scene."

"What's the emotional spine of this love story, and how can I capture it in 2000 words?"

"Rewrite this multi-chapter arc into a single emotionally charged short story."

The trick is *implication*. In a short story, you don't need to *explain* the entire history. You just need to *suggest* it.

One line of dialogue can imply a year of unspoken love. One glance can hint at betrayal. One quiet touch can carry more weight than a page of exposition.

You're not minimizing the story. You're *concentrating* it.

This is especially powerful when you're submitting to anthologies or building a collection. A short Romantasy story that lands with full emotion in a small space can hit just as hard as a novel—sometimes harder, because every word matters.

And if you're stuck on the rewrite, ask ChatGPT to give you scaffolding:

"Write a short story based on these key events: forbidden lovers, one is cursed, they meet again, one chooses sacrifice."

"Summarize this Romantasy novel into five emotional beats that can become a short story."

Whether you're expanding or trimming, what matters most is the **emotional impact**. A Romantasy lives and dies by how much the reader *feels*. Not how long it is.

You're not just managing word counts. You're adjusting *scale*—zooming in or out to reveal different layers of the same truth. Sometimes the whole story lives in a single kiss. Sometimes it needs ten chapters of near-misses before it finally happens.

Trust the story to tell you what it wants to be. Then trust yourself to reshape it without losing the spark that made you write it in the first place.

Making Your Fantasy Political Without Losing the Romance

Romantasy loves drama—emotional, magical, and yes, political. Throwing your characters into a world of kingdoms, councils, rebellions, or empires can make their love story feel bigger and more dangerous. But here's the catch: the moment your story starts featuring thrones, bloodlines, uprisings, or treaties, the romance can start to feel like it's being smothered by plot. Suddenly, you're knee-deep in royal edicts and magical legislation, wondering where the chemistry went.

But you don't have to choose between politics and passion. In fact, when handled right, the political stakes *can heighten* the romance. They can make every stolen moment sharper. Every kiss riskier. Every love confession something that could tip the balance of power. The key is making sure the politics don't overshadow the personal—they should serve it.

So how do you do that?

Let's start with the basics: **what's the central conflict of your world?** Is it a monarchy under threat? A caste system controlled by magical bloodlines? A revolution rising against an empire that forbids love across magical divisions?

Once you've identified the key political force in your fantasy world, ask: *How does this directly affect the lovers?* If it doesn't, you've got a background element—not a driving force. But if the politics interfere with, complicate, or even define the romance? Now you've got stakes.

Ask ChatGPT:

"Suggest political structures in a fantasy world that would make a romantic relationship forbidden or dangerous."

"What kind of magical hierarchy could create tension between two lovers from opposite ends of society?"

"How could a character's political duty conflict with their emotional desires in a Romantasy story?"

You're not writing a textbook on government. You're writing about *power and vulnerability*. Politics in Romantasy should touch the heart, not just the world. They should *pressure* the relationship. Maybe the protagonist is engaged to someone else for political alliance. Maybe the love interest is secretly working for the enemy. Maybe there's a prophecy that says their union will doom the kingdom—or save it.

Once you've defined the tension, **weave it into every romantic beat**. Don't set the politics aside when your characters are alone. Let it bleed into their private moments. A love letter passed under threat of execution. A moment of honesty behind enemy lines. A kiss with spies watching. Politics become more than worldbuilding—they become *emotional weight*.

You can use ChatGPT to brainstorm emotionally layered scenes like this:

"Write a scene where a crown prince confesses love to someone his kingdom would never accept."

"Give me a moment where the lovers realize they're being used as political pawns—and it changes everything."

"Describe an argument between two lovers on opposite sides of a magical war, where both are right."

Political tension isn't just about law and power—it's about *values*. That's where the good stuff lives. What if one lover believes in peace at all costs, while the other thinks the only answer is rebellion? What if one sees magic as a divine right, while the other thinks it corrupts absolutely? Their love becomes a bridge over a moral divide.

These divides make for *real conflict*. And conflict makes romance meaningful.

It also gives your characters a **greater arc**. They don't just grow in their relationship—they grow as people navigating a complicated world. Maybe they start out trying to change the system for love. Maybe they end up changing themselves in the process.

Now, here's where you need to be careful. Don't let the political plotline become a maze. If readers need a flowchart to follow the story, the romance will get buried. Keep your political world elegant, not bloated. Every element should serve either *the characters* or *the romance*—ideally both.

Try this prompt:

"How can I simplify a political Romantasy plot to focus more on emotional consequences?"

"What elements of a rebellion storyline could echo the arc of a forbidden love story?"

"List ways to connect political decisions with relationship milestones."

Also, let romance *change* the politics. Maybe love inspires your character to challenge the system. Or maybe falling for someone on the other side forces them to confront uncomfortable truths. Love doesn't just survive in a political world—it *shakes it up*.

Let's say your protagonist is a royal betrothed to a noble family for power consolidation, but they fall for a mage born in exile. That romance isn't a distraction—it becomes the *core rebellion* of the story. Their bond becomes the wedge that breaks tradition. That's Romantasy done right.

Another way to keep the romance alive? **Anchor the political in the personal**. Readers might not care about the treaty—but they *will* care about the moment your character has to choose between signing it or saving the person they love. They may not track every faction—but they'll hang on to the tension when your lovers end up on opposite sides of a battlefield, neither willing to strike first.

Use politics as a *magnifying glass* for emotional stakes.

Even little touches can carry this weight. A shared symbol of power, like a royal crest, hidden inside a lover's cloak. A secret passage once used for espionage now used for midnight meetings. A public speech written to rally troops that ends up being a coded love letter.

Politics in Romantasy is at its best when it *feels like fate closing in* on love—and love pushing back.

ChatGPT can help brainstorm structure too:

"Give me a three-act Romantasy outline where a political marriage unravels because of forbidden love."

"Suggest midpoint twists that tie a magical coup directly into a romantic arc."

"What political consequences might occur after two lovers break an ancient treaty with a kiss?"

In the end, the trick is **integration**. The politics should push the romance. The romance should push back against the politics. If you can keep that push-pull alive, your story will feel both epic and intimate—just the way Romantasy should.

Love and Gender in Fantasy: Playing With Norms or Breaking Them

Romantasy gives you a blank page—and not just for your story's setting, magic, and lore. It also gives you the rare opportunity to *rebuild the rules of love itself.* In the real world, ideas about gender roles, relationships, and sexuality come with baggage—centuries of culture, law, and expectation. But fantasy lets you sweep all that away if you want to. Or challenge it. Or twist it until it becomes something bold and fresh.

So the question isn't *should* your story play with gender norms—it's *how far do you want to go?*

Some writers stick with familiar dynamics. Others blow them wide open. Some do both, showing a "traditional" kingdom on one side of the map and a wildly progressive one on the other. Some use fantasy to mirror real-world issues. Others use it to dream of a world where those issues *never existed at all.*

There's no single right way to do it. But there is one thing that matters in every version: intention.

Let's start by looking at **gender roles in romance.**

A lot of classic romance tropes are built on very specific roles: the brooding hero, the pure-hearted heroine, the alpha male protector, the beautiful healer. And while those can still be fun in Romantasy, they become *way more interesting* when you flip them—or at least question them.

What if your emotionally repressed hero is the one who needs saving? What if your heroine is a knight in armor who's terrified of intimacy? What if your nonbinary spellcaster is the only one who sees through all the courtly deception and plays the game better than anyone else?

The magic of fantasy is that gender doesn't have to limit how characters act, love, lead, or fight. You get to decide what roles mean in your world.

Ask ChatGPT:

"Give me Romantasy character ideas that defy traditional gender expectations."

"Suggest a romantic arc where a female character is emotionally guarded and the male character is emotionally open."

"Describe a fantasy society where gender roles are reversed or irrelevant—and how that would impact a love story."

You might also want to think about **how gender is defined** in your world at all. Is it binary? Fluid? Tied to magical abilities? Completely divorced from appearance or biology? Maybe your world has more than two recognized genders. Maybe it has none. Maybe gender is something that changes with age, seasons, or spells.

The key isn't to just make a list of cool ideas. It's to tie those choices *into the emotional core* of your story.

If your character lives in a world where they're forced to suppress who they are, how does that shape their capacity to love? If they live in a world where gender doesn't define anything, what does that allow them to explore in their relationships?

Romantasy is also a great space to explore **queer love stories** in ways that feel affirming, magical, and epic. You don't need to explain why a prince can fall in love with another prince—or why a forest spirit uses they/them pronouns. You just *show it*. You normalize it in your world the same way you normalize dragons or soul-bonding or shadow magic.

Fantasy doesn't need to justify inclusivity. It just needs to honor it.

Try prompts like:

"Write a Romantasy meet-cute between a non-binary mage and a royal guard who's never questioned tradition—until now."

"Describe a slow-burn romance between two women in a society where their love is magical but taboo."

"What kind of magical bond might exist in a world that recognizes three genders?"

You can also build **societies** around love and relationships that don't resemble our own. Maybe your world believes in soul-trios instead of soulmates. Maybe relationships are arranged by magical compatibility, not gender. Maybe people express romantic interest with tattoos, rituals, or shared dreams rather than flirtation.

All of these details *reshape the love story*. And they give your world texture that feels lived-in and real.

If you're dealing with a society that *does* have oppressive gender norms, you can use your story to challenge them. A character might rise through a male-dominated order by sheer will and brilliance. Another might hide their true identity for safety. Another might leave their home entirely to live where they can be loved for who they are.

In these stories, the romance becomes *resistance*. It becomes healing. It becomes a declaration that love matters more than power or control.

But if your world is more utopian, your characters might never have to *fight* to be who they are. And that's powerful, too. Because sometimes the most radical thing you can do is show queer, fluid, or unconventional characters *living full lives without trauma*. Falling in love. Making mistakes. Growing.

You can use ChatGPT to imagine both paths:

"Create a Romantasy plot about a character breaking free from their society's gender expectations in order to love freely."

"Suggest a fantasy world where gender doesn't exist, and describe how romance works between characters."

"Write a scene where two characters discover they're soul-bonded—but one has been hiding their true gender."

The beauty of Romantasy is that it lets you *play*. You can build a society where love is telepathic and gender is felt, not seen. You can write a story where the power dynamic has nothing to do with masculine or feminine energy, but with who's willing to be vulnerable first. You can have a warrior queen and a shy healer prince. A chaotic enchanter and a grounded, gruff librarian. You can let love be messy, magical, soft, hard, bright, dark—without being boxed in.

And readers *want* that. They want new kinds of heroes. New kinds of love stories. New ways to feel seen.

You don't have to check every box. Just ask: *Is this character's gender or role being shaped by old defaults—or am I writing something that feels honest, bold, and alive?*

Whether you're subtly shifting expectations or flipping the whole table, make sure every choice deepens the emotional truth of your story. Romance in fantasy doesn't have to follow the same paths we've seen a hundred times. You get to blaze your own.

Creating New Mythologies and Religions That Shape Love and Fate

In Romantasy, the past is never just the past. It echoes in the present, shaping beliefs, destinies, curses, and love itself. Mythologies and religions aren't just background flavor—they're powerful storytelling tools. They whisper truths, lies, and half-remembered prophecies that give your love story a sense of fate. A kiss under a blood moon isn't just romantic—it's been foretold. A forbidden bond isn't just difficult—it's a challenge to the gods.

Creating your own mythologies and spiritual systems allows you to build a world where love isn't just personal—it's *cosmic*. You can make your characters' relationship feel like the result of ancient stories, sacred cycles, or divine mistakes. The trick is to make these beliefs feel *lived in*, *felt*, and *emotionally charged*—not just dumped in exposition.

Start by asking a few big questions:

What does your world believe about love?

Who controls fate—gods, magic, ancestors, stars?

Is love seen as sacred, dangerous, selfish, divine, or something else entirely?

Once you know what your world *believes*, you can start shaping your characters around that belief. Maybe your heroine was raised to believe love is a distraction from duty. Maybe your love interest is marked by a prophecy that says his partner will die young. Maybe soulmates are real—but forbidden by the priesthood.

Use ChatGPT to brainstorm:

"Describe a fantasy religion where romantic love is considered a divine act."

"Give me a mythology about twin stars who fell in love but were cursed to orbit each other forever."

"Create a sacred story that explains why soulbonding is rare and feared."

The best mythologies in Romantasy are *emotionally symbolic*. They don't just explain how the moon got in the sky—they explain why a character is terrified to open their heart. They mirror the inner lives of your characters.

Let's say your world has a legend about a goddess of war and a god of healing who loved each other so fiercely that they destroyed the balance of magic. That myth could play out again in your main couple—maybe one is a fierce protector, the other a quiet nurturer. And maybe they fear they'll repeat that divine mistake.

Suddenly, every glance between them carries more weight.

Also ask: how does the world *practice* these beliefs? Do people pray to a god of heartbreak to help them forget someone? Do lovers carve each other's names into sacred trees? Do weddings involve magical binding rites—or warnings disguised as blessings?

These customs make your world *breathe*. And they let you *show*, not tell, what love means in this society.

You can deepen your ideas by asking ChatGPT:

"What religious rituals could be built around protecting love from dark magic?"

"Suggest a holy festival where people confess secret love under starlight."

"Give me a prophecy format that foretells the rise of two lovers who will change everything."

Mythologies also give you power over *fate*. Prophecies, omens, sacred texts—they let you plant the idea that this love is *meant to be*... or *never should have happened*. Maybe a child was born under the wrong constellation and is doomed to break hearts. Maybe an oracle once said, "Love will end the line of kings." What happens when your protagonist finds themselves tangled in those threads?

You don't have to make the prophecy clear-cut. In fact, Romantasy *loves* a vague, double-edged prophecy. It creates tension. Your characters don't know if their love will save the world or destroy it. And that question will haunt every choice they make.

Let ChatGPT help you write layered prophecies:

"Write a Romantasy prophecy that could mean either salvation or doom, depending on interpretation."

"Create a religious verse that hints at forbidden love but sounds hopeful to those who believe in it."

"Suggest a mythical story about star-crossed lovers that repeats itself every century."

What's especially rich in Romantasy is using mythology not just as plot fuel, but as *emotional background noise*. If a character was raised on a tragic love myth, that shapes how they understand romance. If they were taught that true love always requires sacrifice, they'll carry that belief into every relationship.

And if they decide to *reject* that mythology—if they decide they're going to love someone *anyway*—it's one of the most powerful character turns you can write.

Maybe your lovers have to rewrite the myth by surviving what no one else did. Maybe they prove the gods wrong. Maybe they *are* the reincarnation of a lost legend, and no one realizes it until it's too late.

Fantasy gives you the tools. Romance gives you the heart. Mythology ties it all together.

You can also invent **pantheons** of gods or spirits that reflect the spectrum of love. A god of longing. A goddess of devotion. A spirit of jealousy. A demon of seduction. Let these figures influence the world's rituals—and your characters' fears.

Think about how people invoke these figures. Do they wear certain colors when in mourning for lost love? Do they leave offerings to ensure fidelity? Do rebels tattoo the names of forbidden lovers as an act of protest against divine law?

These details make your world feel emotionally textured. They tell readers: this is a place where love is not just a feeling—it's a force.

One warning: don't overexplain. Let the mythology whisper through dreams, old songs, street graffiti, lullabies, stained glass windows, and half-remembered stories. Let readers feel the myth under the surface of the romance.

And when it's time for a key moment in your plot—like a vow, a betrayal, a death, or a reunion—tie it back to the myth. Let that ancient story wrap around the present one and give it weight.

Because when your love story echoes something timeless—even if it's something *you* made up—it feels bigger. It feels *destined*.

That's the beauty of building your own mythologies and religions. You don't just shape a fantasy world. You shape what love *means* in that world. You give it consequence. You give it legacy. You give it the kind of magic that readers feel in their bones.

Setting the Mood: How to Use Weather, Light, and Time of Day

Mood is everything in Romantasy. It's what makes the air between two characters feel electric without a single word being spoken. It's what makes a kiss under torchlight feel sacred—or dangerous. And while dialogue, emotion, and plot carry the story, the mood *wraps it all in feeling*.

One of the easiest and most powerful ways to control that feeling is with something deceptively simple: **weather, light, and time of day**. These aren't just background details—they're emotional cues. Tools. Symbols. Signals to the reader about *how to feel* in a scene. And when you use them intentionally, they can elevate a moment from pretty good to utterly unforgettable.

Let's start with **weather**.

Rain doesn't just get clothes wet. It slows everything down. It creates quiet. It adds tension. Two people standing in the rain—soaked, shivering, staring at each other—feels completely different than two people sitting on a sunny hillside. Rain can be romantic, tragic, cleansing, oppressive. It can hide tears, drown words, or wash away shame.

You can ask ChatGPT:

"Describe a Romantasy scene where two characters argue in a sudden thunderstorm—heightening their emotional conflict."

"Write a moment of quiet connection during snowfall that softens a character who usually pushes others away."

"Suggest ways fog could symbolically mirror romantic uncertainty."

In fantasy especially, weather can even respond to magic or emotion. Maybe storms roll in when one character is angry or heartbroken. Maybe the sky clears when they touch for the first time. Maybe unnatural weather patterns are tied to a forbidden relationship. Suddenly, the environment *feels* what the characters feel.

Next up: **light**.

The way light behaves in a scene completely changes the tone. Candlelight makes everything intimate. Shadows make things secret. Harsh sunlight can feel judgmental or revealing. A moonlit path? Now you're in poetic territory. Light lets you *shape the emotional contour* of a moment.

Try this: picture a character revealing a painful secret in full daylight. Now imagine them whispering it at dusk, golden light fading from their face. One version feels exposed. The other feels vulnerable. Both work—but they say different things.

Use ChatGPT like this:

"Rewrite this love confession scene to take place in near darkness, with only the glow of fireflies around them."

"Describe how a shaft of moonlight could reveal something magical about a character's true form."

"Suggest lighting details for a Romantasy kiss that takes place in a cathedral lit by stained glass at dawn."

You can even build your world's magic around light. Maybe a certain kind of illumination reveals hidden emotions. Maybe shadows cloak true intentions. Maybe love spells only work when cast at the blue hour—when the sun is just about to vanish and the world feels suspended in breath.

Now let's talk about **time of day**.

Time affects everything—from pacing to tension to symbolism. A dawn meeting feels like a beginning. A midday confrontation feels exposed. A sunset moment feels like an ending, or a choice. And night? That's where things go unspoken. Where people sneak, risk, confess, hide, or give in.

Some of the most emotionally charged scenes in Romantasy happen *after dark*. Not because of sex or secrecy, but because night naturally lowers our guard. There's space to say the things we wouldn't say in daylight. It feels safer. Or scarier. Or more intimate.

Ask ChatGPT:

"Describe a Romantasy scene at dawn where one character is leaving, and the other is pretending not to care."

"What emotions are evoked when a forbidden couple meets at midnight in a sacred grove?"

"Rewrite this argument scene to take place just before sunrise, with both characters exhausted and raw."

Time of day can also be used **symbolically**. A relationship that begins in the dark and ends in light suggests hope. A romance that peaks at sunset and fades into night suggests something bittersweet. You're giving the reader a subconscious map—not with words, but with *atmosphere*.

Want to make it richer? Combine weather, light, and time into a single emotional beat.

Let's say it's dusk. A storm is breaking. The characters are soaked, standing at the edge of a cliff, arguing. But the clouds part just as one of them confesses what they've been hiding all along—and a golden sliver of sun lights their face. Now you've got tension, symbolism, romance, and catharsis—all in the sky and the light.

Here's another: a character wakes before dawn, heart aching. The stars are still out. A cold mist clings to everything. They wander the palace gardens alone, thinking of the one they left behind. That scene *feels* like heartbreak—before a word is spoken.

When you're building mood, think of the setting as another voice in the scene. Not just a silent witness—but an emotional participant.

And if you're stuck? Let ChatGPT help:

"Give me five ideas for how to use time of day to heighten romantic tension."

"Describe a Romantasy world where the weather changes based on people's emotional energy."

"Suggest lighting cues for a scene where a character realizes they're in love but can't say it."

Using weather, light, and time intentionally doesn't just help readers *see* the scene—it helps them *feel* it. These are your director's tools. Your emotional soundtrack. They turn a line of dialogue into a moment that lingers in memory.

So the next time your characters are about to kiss, argue, walk away, or choose each other—ask yourself not just what they say or do, but *what the sky is doing*. What shadows are stretching across the floor. What hour it is, and why it matters.

Because in Romantasy, the world isn't just where the story happens. It *feels* the story too.

From Prompts to Chapters: Letting ChatGPT Surprise You

You don't always have to know everything before you begin. In fact, some of the best Romantasy moments come from a place of curiosity, not control. That's where ChatGPT becomes more than just a helpful assistant—it becomes a co-creator, a spark in the dark, the whisper of a story you didn't know you wanted to tell until it appeared on the page.

Letting ChatGPT surprise you means being open to spontaneity. To discovery. It means using prompts not just to get answers, but to provoke *possibility*.

Because sometimes, what you think is just a throwaway idea turns into a scene so emotionally loaded it makes you stop writing and just *feel*. And sometimes a vague prompt like "Write a magical forest kiss" becomes a full-blown chapter that changes the arc of your entire story.

So how do you turn a prompt into a chapter?

Start with **emotional intention**, not plot. Instead of asking ChatGPT, "What should happen next?", try asking, "What does my protagonist *need* to feel next?" Do they need to trust? To grieve? To resist? To surrender?

Prompt ChatGPT with emotional clarity:

"Write a Romantasy scene where a guarded character lets someone in for the first time."

"Describe a moment of magical intimacy that neither character fully understands—but can't deny."

"Give me a scene where the love interest walks away, believing it's the right thing, even though it hurts."

These prompts don't just give you paragraphs. They give you *opportunities*. You can build an entire chapter around one charged moment like that. And because you didn't plan it—because it surprised you—it often lands more authentically on the page.

Another way to work: give ChatGPT a prompt that's *unfinished*, and let it show you where it could go.

"What would happen if two rival mages accidentally soul-bonded in a fight?"

"How might a character respond if they find out the prophecy wasn't about them—but the one they love?"

"Describe a Romantasy world where love letters written in moonlight reveal your true feelings, even if you lie."

You're not looking for perfect writing right away. You're looking for something that clicks emotionally. When it does, that's your seed. You grow a chapter from it. Add your style, your voice, your character depth—but let the initial spark come from being willing to ask *what if* and see what answers arrive.

And don't stop at scenes. ChatGPT can surprise you with *structure* too. If you're stuck in the middle of your novel, ask:

"Suggest a twist that would force the lovers to question everything they've built together."

"What kind of midpoint decision could make this slow-burn romance finally ignite?"

"Write a moment of false victory that turns into heartbreak."

One of the best ways to generate full chapters is to take a basic beat—say, a reunion after betrayal—and layer it.

Start with:

"Write a Romantasy reunion scene between two characters who haven't seen each other since one betrayed the other."

Then deepen it:

"Add internal thoughts for the character who was betrayed—she's angry but still loves him."

"Give me setting details that heighten the tension—maybe they meet in a sacred place neither expected."

"Rewrite this with more longing and restraint—neither of them wants to say too much."

Before you know it, you've got a chapter with layers: action, dialogue, emotion, setting, conflict. All born from a single idea and a few well-aimed prompts.

Letting ChatGPT surprise you doesn't mean giving up control. It means letting the unexpected *feed* your creativity. It's like improv with a very patient partner. You throw out a feeling, a situation, a line—and ChatGPT throws something back. Sometimes you'll use it exactly. Sometimes it just helps you find your own version.

This back-and-forth can be especially powerful when writing **out of order**. You don't have to write Chapter 1 before Chapter 2. You can write the final confession first. Or the moment everything falls apart. Use prompts like:

"Write the emotionally climactic scene of a Romantasy where the love interest finally reveals his curse."

"What kind of secret could a heroine reveal in Chapter 18 that changes how we saw her in Chapter 3?"

"Give me the last paragraph of a Romantasy where the lovers reunite after years apart."

Once you write those anchor scenes, you can *build backwards or forward*. And the rest of your chapters begin to shape themselves. You're not filling in blanks. You're following emotional echoes.

And when in doubt? Go weird. Go random. Let ChatGPT throw something strange at you and see how you react.

"Write a Romantasy scene where the lovers speak through magical mirrors that distort emotion."

"Give me a dream sequence that reveals a hidden truth about the protagonist's childhood."

"Suggest a magical creature that forces characters to speak only the truth for a single night."

Even if it doesn't end up in the final draft, the exercise might open a new door in the story. And sometimes, one weird little moment becomes the heart of your whole book.

The most important thing is to treat ChatGPT like a *creative partner*, not a vending machine. Don't just press a button and accept whatever drops. Ask again. Shape it. Push deeper. Ask for rewrites in a different tone, a different point of view, a tighter emotional focus.

Let the surprises sharpen your intention.

Romantasy is made of longing and wonder. Surprise is part of that wonder. And ChatGPT can help you get there—not by replacing your creativity, but by feeding it. Prompt by prompt. Page by page. Scene by scene.

So the next time you sit down to write a chapter and you're not sure where to start, try this:

"Show me something beautiful, sad, and a little bit magical—between two people who don't know if they can love each other yet."

And see where it leads.

Writing a Scene That Feels Like a Spell Was Cast on the Reader

There's a kind of scene in Romantasy that doesn't just move the plot forward. It *enchants*. The reader falls into it and forgets to blink. The moment lingers, shimmers, haunts. It's the kind of scene that feels like time stopped—or changed. A kiss in the middle of a snowstorm. A whispered promise in a dream. A look across a battlefield that means everything.

When readers say, "That scene felt like a spell was cast on me," they don't mean it was flashy or dramatic. They mean it *moved them*. It felt personal, poetic, cinematic, and just a little bit magical. Writing a scene like that is about layering emotion, imagery, pacing, and silence until the reader doesn't just see the moment—they *feel it humming in their chest*.

Let's talk about how to create that kind of enchantment, step by step.

Start with **intention**. What is the emotional center of this scene? Not what happens—but what it *means*. Maybe it's the first time your protagonist allows herself to be truly seen. Maybe it's a moment of aching separation, or a brush of fingers that says more than a speech. The stronger the emotional clarity, the more powerful the spell.

Now think about **pacing**. A spellbinding scene isn't rushed. It breathes. Time stretches. You zoom in on details. You slow down to capture every flicker of tension. The reader feels like they're holding their breath—not because of what's happening, but because *how* it's unfolding.

Use white space. Short sentences. Lingering phrases. One-word paragraphs.

Then bring in **sensory detail**. But not just any detail—*specific*, emotionally charged ones. What does the candlelight look like on their skin? What does the cold wind whisper through the trees? What does magic taste like when it hangs in the air before a kiss?

Here's where ChatGPT becomes your spellbook. Try prompts like:

"Write a Romantasy scene where two characters stand on opposite sides of a magical threshold, unable to cross, but desperate to touch."

"Describe the silence between two lovers after a betrayal—but make the tension feel sacred, not just painful."

"Give me imagery for a romantic moment that feels suspended in time—like the world disappeared except for them."

A great spell-scene is full of **metaphor and emotional resonance**. You're not just describing what's happening. You're describing what it *feels like*, even if that feeling doesn't make logical sense.

A heartbeat might sound like thunder. A kiss might feel like falling into the sky. Their name might feel like a truth the character forgot they knew.

Push ChatGPT for poetic language:

"Give me a metaphor for love that feels dangerous but irresistible."

"Rewrite this paragraph using language that evokes magic and longing without using the word 'magic' or 'longing.'"

"How might a character describe the feeling of realizing they've been in love all along—but were too afraid to say it?"

And don't underestimate **silence.** Often, what *isn't* said carries more weight than what is. The most spellbinding scenes usually aren't full of exposition. They're *felt.* A look. A breath. A hesitation. A moment when a hand almost reaches for another—and stops.

You don't have to fill the silence. You have to honor it.

Another tool? **Repetition.** When used sparingly, it creates rhythm. Resonance. It makes a scene feel like a song or a ritual. Repeating a line or image—at the beginning and end of a scene—can create emotional echoes that linger long after the chapter ends.

Let's look at an example. A character remembers a story their mother once told: "When the moon turns red, true love reveals itself." Maybe they don't believe it. Maybe they scoff. But then, later in the book, they stand in front of the person they've tried not to love—and above them, the moon glows crimson. That moment doesn't need explanation. It's a *spell* that was cast earlier—and now blooms.

You can even *build toward* a spellbinding scene throughout your book. Seed it with quiet foreshadowing. A shared memory. A piece of music. A whispered phrase. Then bring those elements together in a moment of emotional release. That's how you write scenes that feel destined—because you've been weaving the threads since chapter one.

Ask ChatGPT:

"Suggest a repeated line or symbol that can quietly appear throughout a Romantasy novel—then pay off emotionally in a late chapter."

"What kind of object or ritual could symbolize a secret love between two characters over time?"

"Give me ways to make a seemingly small gesture—like brushing hair away from a face—feel momentous."

These kinds of scenes don't need battles or declarations. They need *truth.* And vulnerability. And the courage to let stillness carry meaning.

Sometimes the spell is cast by a literal enchantment. A memory-sharing spell. A magical veil that drops. A dream they didn't know they shared. You can use the fantasy element to heighten the intimacy—but only if the emotional core is already strong.

The magic supports the moment. It doesn't replace it.

The goal is to leave the reader in a quiet emotional daze when they finish the scene. That moment when they close the book and just sit there, not ready to turn the page. Not because they're confused—but because they're *changed*, even if only a little.

That's what a spell feels like.

And you don't have to do it every chapter. You only need a few of these moments in a book. But those few? They're the ones readers highlight. Quote. Share. Cry over. Reread.

They're the moments that make your Romantasy unforgettable.

So the next time you reach a pivotal scene, don't rush to write what happens.

Pause.

Ask: *What needs to be felt here?*

What's the light doing?

What are they afraid to say?

What's the one line that could break the silence—or seal it?

What's the magic—literal or emotional—at work in this moment?

Then let the words come slowly. Let them shimmer. Let them breathe.

Let them cast a spell.

Designing Magical Items or Places That Reflect Emotional Truth

Every great Romantasy has that *one thing* you can picture long after you've closed the book. A mirror that shows the heart's desire. A grove where lovers leave offerings no one else can see. A necklace that glows when two people miss each other. These aren't just magical flourishes. They're *symbols*, tied directly to the emotional truth of the story.

The most powerful magical items or places in Romantasy don't just serve the plot—they serve the *feeling*. They reflect something hidden, aching, or unspoken within the characters. That's the secret. You're not creating a cool magical thing. You're creating a metaphor with weight.

So, where do you start?

Start with emotion. What is your protagonist struggling to express or understand? What do they fear? Long for? Regret? That emotional core is your blueprint.

Let's say your main character is terrified of intimacy. You could create a magical ring that lets someone feel what the wearer feels—but only when removed. Now the object becomes a loaded symbol. When they finally take it off, it's not just about magic—it's a gesture of *emotional exposure*. That's the kind of moment readers remember.

Ask ChatGPT:

"Suggest magical objects that could represent emotional vulnerability in a Romantasy story."

"Create a place that reflects the love between two characters but is slowly fading."

"Give me a magical artifact that reveals how two people truly feel about each other—but only once."

Another example: imagine a tree that blooms only when someone speaks their truest thought. Or a necklace that shatters when a promise is broken. Or a library that lets you relive a memory—but only if you're willing to feel it again completely.

These aren't plot devices. They're emotional truths, externalized. They let the characters *interact* with what they feel in a physical, magical way.

And they don't need to be obvious. Sometimes the best magical objects are quiet, personal, subtle. A charm that warms in the presence of a soulmate. A lockbox that whispers the name of the person you secretly love when opened. A map that only leads to places you've dreamed of being with someone.

The goal is resonance. That "oh" moment when a reader realizes what the object *means*, not just what it does.

You can also think about magical **places** the same way. A Romantasy world should be full of places where emotions are amplified, exposed, or transformed. Think: the cave where soulbonding rituals are performed. The river that takes memories in exchange for clarity. The garden where every flower represents a different kind of love—loyalty, passion, regret, devotion.

Ask ChatGPT:

"Describe a Romantasy location where characters must confront what they hide from themselves emotionally."

"Create a sacred place where two lovers can speak freely without magical consequences."

"Give me a place that appears differently depending on what the visitor feels most."

What makes these places work is that they don't just exist for scenery—they exist for **emotional evolution.** If a character goes into a sacred chamber full of illusions and walks out unchanged, it doesn't matter how cool the visuals were. But if they leave that space having *chosen* something—truth over comfort, vulnerability over silence—then the place has power.

A beautifully crafted magical item or location should:

- Symbolize a character's emotional journey
- Reflect the story's core theme
- Evolve in meaning as the romance evolves

Let's say you create a locket that opens only when the character truly believes they are loved. Early in the story, it won't open—and that moment stings. Later, maybe the love interest gives it back to them, believing they're not worthy. But when the protagonist finally opens it alone, you've got a metaphor for healing, trust, and self-worth—all packed into one small, magical object.

That's what readers hold on to.

If you're feeling stuck, flip it around. Start with an object or place, and *build the emotion into it.*

Try prompts like:

"Invent a magical artifact and then describe how it could reflect a character's fear of abandonment."

"Give me a location that tests characters emotionally before allowing them to enter."

"Describe a magical item that changes as a relationship deepens."

You don't need hundreds of magical objects or places. Just a few that matter. Ones that appear at the right moments—moments of decision, connection, separation, realization.

Also, don't forget how these magical elements can be **shared** between lovers. A compass that always points to the one you love. A book that fills with notes from both characters, even across distances. A set of bracelets that glow with matching colors depending on what the other person is feeling.

These shared items become *emotional threads* through your narrative. When a character looks down and sees the bracelet flicker red, they know something's wrong. When they open the book and see a message written in their love's handwriting, even after a fight, they *feel it*. It's an anchor.

You can also create magic that *misleads* or *challenges* characters. Maybe there's an artifact said to reveal true love—but what it reveals is the person they're afraid to love. Maybe a shrine that grants one wish at the cost of forgetting a memory—how do you choose between a future and your past?

Use ChatGPT to heighten these ideas:

"Write a Romantasy scene where a character must destroy a magical object that connects them to their soulmate in order to save their world."

"Describe a garden that remembers every kiss and heartbreak that ever happened in its walls."

"Invent a magical ritual where lovers must walk through a mirror of each other's pain before they can bond."

Your goal is to create magic that doesn't just serve the fantasy—but *deepens the feeling.*

Readers don't remember stats, mechanics, or lore unless it makes them feel something. What they remember is the soft pulse of a ring warming in the pocket of a hero who thought they were alone. Or the moment a door opens not with a key, but with a confession.

The best magical objects and places in Romantasy don't tell us how the world works. They tell us how the characters *feel.* And when they're done right, it's like casting a spell the reader doesn't even know they're under—until their heart tightens just a little and they realize: *this means something.*

Love Triangles, Soul Bonds, and Destiny: Classic Fantasy Devices

There are a few storytelling devices in Romantasy that readers come back for again and again, no matter how many times they've seen them. Love triangles. Soul bonds. Destiny. They're the emotional fireworks of fantasy romance—the tropes that make hearts pound and fingers turn pages long past midnight.

But for all their popularity, these devices can go wrong fast if they're treated like clichés or crutches. The trick is to use them with emotional weight, thoughtful intention, and just enough unpredictability to make them feel *new*, even if the bones are familiar.

Let's talk about each one and how to make it not just work—but resonate.

Love triangles are often misunderstood. People think they're about choosing between two lovers. But what they're really about is *internal conflict made external.* It's not just "Who will they choose?" It's "Who am I when I'm with each of them?" One love interest might represent safety, history, or who the character used to be. The other might represent risk, transformation, or who they're becoming.

When you frame a triangle this way, it becomes more than a game of romantic ping-pong. It becomes an emotional crossroads. And that's when readers care.

Ask ChatGPT:

"Write a Romantasy love triangle where one suitor reflects the protagonist's past, and one reflects their future."

"Suggest reasons a protagonist might feel torn between two characters without making either of them a villain."

"What kinds of magical consequences could arise from choosing one love over another?"

Love triangles also get better when they involve more than romance. Maybe there's political tension. Maybe choosing one side means betraying the other in battle. Maybe the love interests are soulbound to opposing magical factions. That added tension raises the stakes.

And speaking of **soul bonds**—here's where Romantasy gets that mystical edge. The idea that two people are magically, spiritually, or cosmically tied together has deep appeal. Soul bonds promise intensity. Fate. Unbreakable connection.

But if you want your soul bond to *hit*, you can't let it do all the work for the romance. Just because two characters are bonded doesn't mean they like each other. In fact, some of the best soul bond stories are the ones where the characters actively *resist* it. They're bonded—but they don't want to be. Or they do—but one of them is afraid.

Soul bonds should create pressure, not resolution. They raise questions like:

What if I don't want to love you?

What if you die and I feel it?

What if this bond ruins everything else?

Those questions make it interesting. They turn the soul bond from a convenience into a conflict.

Use ChatGPT to explore angles like:

"Describe a Romantasy soul bond that forms between two enemies—and they try to break it."

"What kind of emotional or physical consequences could happen if a soul bond is ignored?"

"Create a magical ceremony for soul bonding that reflects fear as well as love."

You can also make soul bonds imperfect. Maybe they reveal emotions, but only partially. Maybe they don't activate until trust is real. Maybe they *fade* when the love fades. A bond doesn't have to be eternal to feel sacred. In fact, making it fragile might give it more depth.

Now, let's tackle **destiny**. Few words are more loaded in Romantasy. It's the idea that a character's fate is written in the stars, in prophecy, in divine law. And sometimes, that fate includes love.

Destiny can be romantic when it's treated as awe, mystery, even burden. The idea that two people were meant for each other can feel magical—but it can also feel *claustrophobic*. Maybe they hate the idea of having no choice. Maybe they wonder if their love is real or just written.

The best Romantasy destinies aren't about "everything was always going to happen this way." They're about choice. The moment a character says, *I could walk away—but I won't.* That's when destiny becomes powerful.

Use prompts like:

"Write a scene where a character realizes they've been falling in love with someone the prophecy warned them against."

"Describe a destiny that promises great love but comes at a terrible cost."

"What kind of prophecy might be misunderstood for most of the story, and only make sense after a romantic choice is made?"

You can also *break* destiny. Maybe the whole story has pointed toward one outcome—and then the character refuses it. Or maybe they fulfill it, but in a way no one expected. That twist gives agency back to the characters and makes the payoff satisfying.

Want to go even deeper? Combine these devices.

Imagine a soul bond between two people—and then a prophecy that says one must die. Or a love triangle where one character is soul-bound to the protagonist, but the protagonist's *true* feelings lie with the other. Or maybe the soul bond isn't even romantic—it's formed with someone the protagonist doesn't love, which makes loving someone else complicated or even dangerous.

These combinations keep the tropes from feeling tired. They create new emotional shapes for the reader to explore.

And of course, ChatGPT is your ally here. You can test dozens of variations until something clicks. Try:

"Build a Romantasy triangle where one character is soulbound, and another shares a magical dream connection."

"List five prophecy ideas that create tension between love and duty."

"Give me character arcs for three people caught in a soul bond triangle that doesn't resolve the way readers expect."

The goal isn't to avoid these classic devices. It's to *embrace them*—but with clarity, purpose, and emotion.

These tropes work because they go deep. They reflect real human fears and longings. We all wonder what would happen if we had to choose between comfort and passion. We all dream of someone knowing us completely. We all feel the pull of fate—and the thrill of rewriting it.

So use them. Bend them. Break them. And let your Romantasy be as grand, tender, messy, and magical as it wants to be.

What If They are Not Human? Fantasy Romance across Species

Fantasy opens the door wide to love stories that would be impossible—or at least very weird—in the real world. A mermaid and a prince. A dragon in human form falling for a mage. A mortal girl and a centuries-old fae lord. These aren't just imaginative twists. They're ways of asking deeper questions: What does it mean to love someone different from you? What bridges connection when biology, lifespan, language, or even basic understanding don't line up?

Romancing non-human characters is a staple of Romantasy, but it comes with its own unique magic and challenges. Done right, these stories hit hard. They feel mythic, intense, primal. Done wrong, they can feel flat or even problematic.

So let's talk about how to do it well—and why these kinds of relationships might be the most powerful ones you write.

Start with the question: **Why isn't this character human?**

It's not just about cool wings or glowing eyes. A non-human love interest should reflect something meaningful—something the protagonist lacks, fears, or is drawn to. Maybe they live by a different emotional logic. Maybe they represent a freedom the human character can't imagine. Or maybe their immortality forces the couple to see time—and love—differently.

Ask ChatGPT:

"Describe a Romantasy relationship between a mortal healer and an immortal warrior who fears attachment."

"Create a non-human character whose emotional expression is completely foreign to humans—and explore how this affects romance."

"Write a first meeting between a human protagonist and a telepathic forest creature who doesn't understand individual identity."

Fantasy romance across species thrives on **contrast**. That's what makes the attraction electric. Think about beauty vs. danger, instinct vs. reason, control vs. wildness, fleeting vs. eternal. When your characters come from different worlds—literally or metaphorically—every moment between them hums with tension. And when they connect despite that? It feels like magic because it *is* magic.

But don't fall into the trap of making the non-human character just a sexy costume. They need culture, beliefs, rituals, language, flaws. They're not just a fantasy boyfriend or girlfriend—they're a person with alien values. If they're a shapeshifter, how do they feel about the body? If they live in a hive mind, how do they define intimacy? If they live for 300 years, what does "forever" mean to them?

Use prompts like:

"Describe how a dragon character might express affection differently than a human."

"Create a romantic custom practiced by fae that's considered offensive to humans."

"What challenges would a human face trying to love a creature made of living mist?"

The more *specific* the species and culture, the more your romance will sing. Maybe your vampire doesn't drink blood anymore—but they remember what it was like to hunger for something they couldn't control. Maybe your protagonist is in love with a ghost, and every interaction carries the ache of memory and "touchlessness".

And don't forget the **emotional stakes.** The "I love you" moment in a human-non-human romance should feel heavier. More risky. What happens when one of them can die, and the other can't? Or when one of them sees time in centuries, while the other is racing the clock?

These differences don't have to be obstacles—they can be *the point.* Loving someone different challenges identity. It forces characters to redefine what love is—beyond body, beyond logic, beyond survival.

You can even use physical differences to create intimacy. Not as spectacle, but as vulnerability. Maybe the non-human character is terrified to reveal their true form. Maybe they've been rejected before. Maybe they only shift when they feel safe. The moment they do? That's more powerful than any kiss.

Use ChatGPT to explore emotional resonance:

"Write a Romantasy scene where a character reveals their monstrous true form—and waits to see if they'll be loved anyway."

"Describe a bonding ritual between a human and a creature that communicates through light and color, not words."

"Give me a moment where a non-human character sees the fragility of human life—and chooses to protect it at great cost."

You can also flip expectations. What if the *human* is the terrifying one? What if the magical creature has been warned not to trust humans? What if the love interest fears falling for someone with such a short lifespan, knowing they'll grieve again and again?

Or go deeper into **hybrid identity**. Maybe one character is part human, part something else. Maybe the romance awakens a buried part of their nature. Maybe falling in love means becoming something new—physically, emotionally, magically.

And yes, there's space for **spice** in these stories too—but treat it with care. Think about consent across species. Think about communication. Think about what physical connection means when bodies don't work the same way. There's plenty of room for sensuality—but it's most powerful when it's grounded in emotional connection.

The best interspecies romances aren't about exoticism. They're about recognition. A look that says, *I don't understand you completely—but I want to.* A choice to love someone who doesn't fit into your world. A decision to build a world together anyway.

These stories carry a special kind of resonance. Because at their heart, they're about *difference.* And love in the face of difference is always more compelling than love built on sameness.

Use ChatGPT for worldbuilding like:

"Design a Romantasy world where humans and magical beings coexist uneasily, and falling in love can lead to exile."

"List challenges a human diplomat might face trying to negotiate peace with a telepathic alien species—and falling for one of them."

"Create a fantasy setting where the moon chooses soulmates across species, and society tries to deny the bonds."

At the end of the day, whether your love interest has wings, fur, fangs, gills, or is made entirely of starlight, what matters is that the story feels *true*. The emotional logic should always land. If a human falls in love with a fae queen who can't lie, what does that teach them about honesty? If a forest spirit who's lived a thousand years learns to feel again through one mortal's touch, what does that teach them about time?

The reader may never live in a world with phoenixes or dryads or shapeshifting shadows. But they *will* know what it feels like to fall for someone who sees the world differently. Who doesn't quite belong. Who might leave.

And if you can capture that? You'll cast a spell they won't forget.

Describing Intimacy without Losing the Magic or Taste

Intimacy is one of the most powerful tools in Romantasy—but it's also one of the trickiest. It's the moment where your characters stop posturing and protecting. Where the masks drop. Where the emotional current that's been running under every stolen glance and sharp word finally breaks the surface. But here's the delicate line: how do you write these moments in a way that feels true, beautiful, magical—and never cringey or forced?

Whether your characters are sharing a first kiss, a soul-bonding touch, or something more physical, the goal isn't just to describe bodies or actions. The goal is to *hold the emotion and wonder in the moment*, so the reader doesn't just see it—they *feel it*. That's the magic. That's where the intimacy becomes more than just sensual. It becomes unforgettable.

Let's start with what intimacy really *means* in a Romantasy.

It's not just physical closeness—it's emotional exposure. It's being seen. Being chosen. Sometimes, it's being vulnerable in ways the character never thought they'd allow. Maybe your warrior puts down their sword. Maybe your immortal admits to fear. Maybe your shapeshifter reveals their true form in the moment of connection. These emotional beats matter more than where a hand lands or how long the kiss lasts.

So before you even write the scene, ask:

What has been keeping these characters apart until now?

What does this moment *cost* them to step into?

What does it *change* once it happens?

Now bring in the tone. You don't want the scene to feel clinical or overly flowery. Somewhere between raw truth and poetic restraint is the sweet spot. And ChatGPT can help you get there.

Start with emotional prompts:

"Write a Romantasy scene where two characters share a moment of physical closeness for the first time, but focus on the emotional tension more than the physical act."

"Describe the slow build-up to a kiss that both characters have wanted but feared, making the moment feel suspended in time."

"Write a scene where a magical bond intensifies physical touch, heightening every sensation emotionally and spiritually."

The best intimacy scenes in Romantasy are grounded in *specific sensory detail*—but not just any details. Use details that *mirror what the characters are feeling*. If a character is nervous, maybe they notice the texture of the other's clothing because they're too afraid to meet their eyes. If a character feels overwhelmed, maybe the air suddenly feels thinner, like it's just them in the universe.

Touch doesn't have to be explicit to be powerful. The brush of a thumb across a knuckle. The feeling of someone's breath near your ear. The way time slows when someone whispers your name.

Use ChatGPT to find the language that suits your tone:

"Write a Romantasy scene that describes a kiss in language that's poetic but restrained—no clichés, just vulnerability."

"Create metaphors for intimacy that don't mention fire or electricity, but still carry emotional heat."

"Describe physical closeness through the lens of fear, longing, and awe."

And here's a little secret: **you don't need to describe everything**. In fact, leaving space—those poetic fade-to-blacks or implied touches—can make the scene *more* powerful. You let the reader feel like they're witnessing something private, even sacred.

A well-written moment of intimacy doesn't scream "look at this!" It *invites* the reader in. It says: *you know what this feels like. Feel it with them.*

And if you're writing a scene that goes further than kissing—whether that's magically charged bonding, sensual exploration, or sex—remember, *tone is everything*. What makes a scene feel magical isn't what the characters do. It's how they feel. How they change. How the moment unfolds like a confession of everything they've held back.

Here are ways to approach that through prompts:

"Write a Romantasy scene where two lovers become physically intimate, focusing on emotional tenderness and mutual respect rather than explicit detail."

"Describe a magically induced moment of emotional merging that feels deeply romantic and sensual without being graphic."

"Give me a love scene between two characters who have waited a long time, and who finally allow themselves to be fully known."

Let the intimacy reflect the world you've built. In some Romantasy worlds, maybe physical touch is sacred. Maybe it has magical consequences. Maybe lovers are bound together in ways that change them physically or emotionally forever. Use those rules to heighten the weight of the moment.

Maybe a kiss exchanges memories. Maybe a soul bond forms in the moment of climax. Maybe one lover can see the other's deepest desire during physical connection. These devices add fantasy to intimacy—and give readers something they won't find in a contemporary romance.

But never forget: *consent is part of the magic*. Especially in stories where power imbalances (age, experience, magic, species, rank) might exist. Your characters should choose each other—not just with passion, but with presence.

And always, always let the intimacy feel earned. It should come after emotional connection, not before it. Even if your characters are impulsive, even if they're desperate—there should be *something true* underneath the moment. That's what transforms physical closeness into *emotional depth*.

If you're ever unsure, let ChatGPT test tone for you:

"Rewrite this intimate scene to feel softer and more emotionally vulnerable."

"Make this moment feel sacred rather than erotic."

"Turn this physically charged scene into something quiet and emotionally weighted."

You don't have to write like anyone else. Your Romantasy can be tender, steamy, slow-burn, poetic, awkward, sacred, or wild. What matters is that it feels honest—and that it never loses *the emotional heartbeat* that started it all.

Because in the end, describing intimacy in Romantasy isn't about writing a "love scene."

It's about capturing the moment when the characters stop pretending.

When magic meets vulnerability.

When a kiss says what words couldn't.

When touch means more than touch—it means *truth*.

And when you write that well, readers don't just read it.

They *feel spellbound* by it.

Creating a Series from One Romantasy Tale

You've written your Romantasy story. It's emotional, magical, complete—or is it? The truth is, most great Romantasy worlds *don't want to end*. The characters linger. The magic still hums. The readers ask, "What happens next?" And the smartest thing you can do is listen to that feeling—because it might be the seed of a series.

Creating a series out of a single Romantasy tale doesn't mean you drag a finished story on longer than it should go. It means you *recognize what still pulses underneath the ending*. Loose threads. Expanding lore. Side characters who feel like protagonists in disguise. Magical consequences that haven't fully played out yet. That's your doorway to something bigger.

So how do you take one book and spin it into many—without losing the heart of what made the first story work?

Start by asking what kind of **series structure** fits your story. There are three common shapes Romantasy series take:

1. **A direct continuation** – Book two picks up where book one ended. The couple might face new trials, or their relationship evolves while new threats or mysteries unfold. Think of this as an emotional and plot-based escalation.
2. **A companion series** – Each book focuses on a different couple in the same world. Book one's side characters step into the spotlight. The original protagonists show up occasionally, but the love story centers around someone new.
3. **A generational or legacy series** – The story jumps forward (or backward) in time. A new era. A new magical threat. Maybe a child of the original couple, or someone living with the consequences of their choices.

Each path lets you build *outward* from your original story—but in a way that feels natural, not forced.

Use ChatGPT to brainstorm which path fits best:

"What kind of sequel would deepen the emotional arc of a Romantasy where the couple defied fate to be together?"

"List five side characters from a Romantasy book who could become leads in their own story."

"Describe a world-shaking consequence of a magical love bond that could set up a new series arc."

Next, think about what *wasn't answered* in the original story. Did the magic system leave questions? Was there a larger political or mythical threat in the background? Were there cultural tensions, magical debts, or ancient prophecies that still haven't played out?

Often, your world is richer than your first plot can contain. That's a gift. You can step into those shadows and write a new story that reveals more.

Maybe your protagonist's love story ended happily, but they now rule a kingdom that's crumbling. Maybe the magical bond they forged with their partner has unexpected side effects. Maybe a forgotten god stirs because their love rewrote fate—and now others must pay the price.

Ask ChatGPT:

"Suggest a Romantasy series arc that starts with a personal love story but expands into an epic magical war."

"What kind of world-spanning fallout could come from breaking a sacred romantic prophecy?"

"Describe a magical relic introduced in book one that becomes the central threat in book two."

Another place to look for expansion: **your side characters**. If you created them with real emotional depth and backstory, chances are they have arcs just waiting to unfold. The best companion books come from asking, "What was this character doing while the main story happened—and what's their love story going to cost them?"

Readers love companion books because they return to a familiar world with new emotional stakes. There's comfort *and* discovery.

And don't be afraid to write **romances in different flavors**. If your first book was enemies-to-lovers with lots of angst, maybe your second is a forbidden slow-burn. Or a second-chance romance. You keep the magic and emotional resonance, but give readers a new kind of journey.

Ask ChatGPT:

"Write a teaser for a Romantasy book centered around the original protagonist's rival, now the romantic lead."

"Suggest a redemption romance arc for a character who was the antagonist in book one."

"Give me a character-driven love story in the same world, but from a different magical culture."

You also want to plan for **growth**—both magical and emotional. As your characters change, your world should evolve. Magic deepens. Laws shift. New beings emerge. Maybe a once-minor conflict becomes a looming war. Maybe a new magical threat rises as a reaction to a broken oath from book one. Your story doesn't just continue—it *builds*.

Series storytelling lets you explore deeper themes over time. Maybe book one is about finding love. Book two is about protecting it. Book three is about understanding what you'd give up—or fight for—to keep it. The best Romantasy series don't just rehash—they *transform*.

Another thing to consider: **romantic resolution**. If your original couple had their happily-ever-after, ask if they need to be challenged again. Or if it's time to let them be the emotional anchor while others fall in love. Some readers want their favorite couple back center stage. Others love when the spotlight moves.

There's no wrong answer—just make sure it fits the emotional tone of your series.

You can also have overarching plot threads that tie books together. Maybe there's a legendary magical force that each couple plays a role in awakening. Or a curse that affects the entire world, but each book reveals a new piece of how to break it. The key is to give each book its own emotional arc *and* let it contribute to a larger myth.

Try prompts like:

"Create a five-book Romantasy series outline where each story focuses on a different magical artifact tied to a love story."

"What kind of epic prophecy could bind multiple love stories across generations?"

"Give me a final series-ending scene where the original couple's story comes full circle."

And don't forget—you don't have to plan everything from book one. But planting seeds early helps. That mysterious character who disappears in the middle of book one? Maybe they're your next protagonist. That reference to a magical empire in the east? Maybe it's your next setting.

You're building a world readers want to return to. Let it expand organically, but *with meaning*. Don't write sequels just because. Write them because there's more truth to uncover. More love to test. More wonder to reveal.

Romantasy isn't just about big emotions. It's about *legacy*. A great single book can make a reader swoon. A great series can *change them*. It creates a space they return to, again and again—not because they forget the ending, but because they never wanted it to end at all.

How to Avoid Info Dumps (Even With Complex Worlds)

Worldbuilding is one of the greatest joys of writing Romantasy. You've dreamed up magical systems, ancient histories, ethereal kingdoms, soul bonds, customs, bloodlines, portals, politics—and you want to share it all. Right now. On the first page. But here's the truth: readers don't fall in love with a world because of a massive history lesson. They fall in love with the *feeling* of the world—what it does to the characters, how it breathes into their choices, what it reveals about love, fear, and transformation.

An info dump, no matter how beautifully written, feels like hitting a wall. It stops the story cold. It makes readers feel like students when they came for enchantment. And worst of all? It gets in the way of the romance. So, let's talk about how to *weave* your complex world into your story without dumping it in the reader's lap like an encyclopaedia.

First, understand what an **info dump** really is. It's not just too much information—it's information delivered in the *wrong moment*, in the *wrong format*, for the *wrong reason*. Usually, it happens when the writer tries to explain the world instead of *showing* how it affects the people who live in it.

So here's rule one: always connect information to *emotion*. If you want to explain how soul bonds work, don't start with a paragraph of mechanics. Show a character *fighting* the bond. Show them having nightmares because they feel someone else's pain. Let them explain, "It's the bond—it's tearing me up every time you hurt." And suddenly, the reader gets it. Not just the concept—but the *cost*.

Use ChatGPT like this:

"Write a Romantasy scene where the magical laws of a kingdom are revealed during a conversation between two characters hiding from them."

"Describe the history of a soul bond through a character's memory of a childhood story."

"Show a complex magical system from the perspective of someone who *hates* how it controls their life."

When you frame information as story—not lecture—it *sticks*. And more importantly, it feels earned.

Another way to avoid info dumps is by using **character assumptions**. Don't have two characters explain things to each other they already know. It reads as fake. Instead, show them *reacting to those things*. Maybe your heroine passes a temple and looks away because she doesn't want to think about what happened there. Maybe your love interest mutters an old proverb under his breath—one the reader doesn't fully understand, but feels.

This is called **"leaving gaps on purpose."** Readers don't need to understand everything at once. In fact, mystery draws them in. They'll wait for answers if you give them stakes, emotion, and forward motion.

Ask ChatGPT for strategies like:

"Write a Romantasy scene where the reader learns something about the world *without* the characters talking about it directly."

"Give me ways to imply magical rules through character behavior instead of exposition."

"What kinds of visual or sensory cues can reveal a city's political history in a single paragraph?"

You can also **drip-feed backstory and lore** through dialogue, setting, rituals, and even intimacy. Maybe one character has a scar that glows during certain moon phases—and we don't find out why until they're willing to open up. Maybe a romantic gift is more than it seems—a charm passed down from a forbidden love a hundred years ago.

Use **scene framing** to embed worldbuilding into the atmosphere. Instead of explaining the cultural tradition of midnight confession rituals, *set your next romantic scene inside one*. Instead of telling the reader about a festival, drop the characters into it—smelling the spiced air, dodging flying lanterns, realizing they're alone in a crowd.

Use ChatGPT like this:

"Describe a Romantasy setting where the architecture reveals the magical hierarchy without any exposition."

"Write a kiss scene during a chaotic festival that subtly teaches the reader about the world's social customs."

"Give me small, powerful details that imply the presence of a prophecy without stating it."

Another trick? Let your **characters misunderstand things**. Especially if you're using a character from outside the magical culture as your POV. They might make wrong assumptions. Learn slowly. Ask awkward questions. This gives you an organic way to share information with the reader while keeping the character's voice alive.

Example: your protagonist thinks the glowing river means the city is cursed. The love interest says, "No—it's sacred. That glow? It's memory." That one exchange teaches the reader about the river, the magic, and the character's beliefs—all through dialogue.

And don't underestimate the power of **well-timed metaphor**. Instead of saying "Dragons ruled this kingdom until they were hunted into extinction," let a character say, "My grandfather still flinches at thunder—he says it sounds like wings." One line, all the history you need.

When in doubt, ask yourself this: *Do I need the reader to know this right now—or do I just want them to?*

If it's not essential to the current emotional or plot beat, it can wait. Let the world unfold as the romance deepens. Let the lore rise like mist. Let the reader discover, not digest.

Use ChatGPT as a testing ground:

"Rewrite this paragraph of exposition into a scene with emotional stakes."

"Turn this block of backstory into dialogue that reveals a character's bias."

"Convert this info dump into three separate scenes that show the world naturally."

You can also plan *where* to place your worldbuilding. Early on, use only what you need to ground the reader. As the romance builds, you can expand the lore. As emotional stakes rise, deepen the magic. Let the world grow as the love grows.

In Romantasy, the world and the romance aren't separate. They're woven. What magic does to love. What love changes in the world. What a kiss means when it could end a war—or start one.

So trust your world. Trust your reader. And trust that when the heart is engaged, even the strangest magic will make sense—because it *feels* true.

Using ChatGPT to Create an Entire Fantasy Glossary or Lorebook

At some point in your Romantasy journey, your story world might start spilling beyond the edges of your book. You've got ancient bloodlines, enchanted objects, magical rituals, three kinds of fae, an empire's fall, two moon deities, and a forgotten prophecy that hinges on a single phrase in an extinct language. That's when you know: it's time to build a **glossary or lorebook**.

This isn't about creating a dry index. It's about **making your world feel real**—not just to the reader, but to you. A glossary gives you consistency. A lorebook gives your story roots. And with ChatGPT, you don't have to build it alone. You've got a worldbuilding engine at your fingertips.

Let's walk through how to create a beautifully rich glossary or lorebook with ChatGPT's help—from naming to structure to using it as a living tool while you write.

Start with your **categories**. A fantasy glossary can include:

- Named magical systems
- Races, species, and cultural groups
- Historical events or myths
- Places of importance (kingdoms, cities, sacred locations)
- Magical items or artifacts
- Religions, deities, or belief systems
- Government structures, noble houses, or orders
- Unique romantic customs
- Fantasy terminology or foreign-language terms
- Prophecies, curses, and old sayings

Now you can feed this list to ChatGPT and start building from there:

"Help me organize a glossary for my Romantasy novel. Here are the categories I want to include. Suggest the best order and possible additions."

"I'm creating a lorebook for a Romantasy world. What standard entries should be in it to keep my story consistent across a series?"

Once you have your structure, start populating it. You don't need to invent everything at once. Begin with what's already in your draft. That magical flower that blooms only for true love? That kingdom that fell a hundred years ago? That old fae law that binds two characters together? Those go in first.

If you want to go deeper or expand what you already have, ChatGPT is perfect for brainstorming:

"Write a glossary entry for a magical ritual called The Binding Flame, which joins two soulmates but leaves a burn mark on the heart."

"Create a short myth about the founding of the kingdom of Elaria, where a human queen and a fae prince fell in love and built peace through blood magic."

"Describe a sacred location called the Weeping Vale, where lovers leave offerings to forget past heartbreak."

What makes a fantasy glossary *sparkle* isn't just the facts. It's the tone. Do you want your lorebook to read like ancient scrolls? A whispered oral history? A scholar's collection? A lover's diary? You can ask ChatGPT to rewrite entries in different voices and see what fits your world best.

"Rewrite this glossary entry as if spoken by a cynical court historian who doesn't believe in romance."

"Make this description of a magical object sound poetic, like a bedtime story passed through generations."

"Create contrasting entries about the same event—one from the human perspective, and one from the fae."

This not only builds richness—it introduces *unreliable narrators*. Not every entry needs to be objective. Some can be rumors. Legends. Biased retellings. And that creates delicious ambiguity your main story can play with.

Once you've got a batch of entries, think about **format**. Are you building an appendix for your novel? A separate companion guide? An in-world artifact your characters reference (like a grimoire or codex)? You can use ChatGPT to help design the right tone and structure for each.

"Format this list of magical orders into a clean glossary entry with names, ranks, and symbols."

"Write an excerpt from a Romantasy grimoire describing the spell 'Heartglow' and its side effects."

"Create a traveler's field guide entry about mythical beasts that appear only when people are in love."

Another powerful tool: **cross-referencing**. Good lorebooks give readers the sense that everything is connected. A kingdom's founding myth might link to a current prophecy. A forbidden romance from the past might echo in your protagonist's story. You can build internal connections with prompts like:

"Link these five glossary entries together through a shared legend or symbol."

"Describe how the moon deity Selune influences the laws of love in different kingdoms."

"Create a prophecy that references at least three other glossary entries from this Romantasy world."

And here's the real magic: your glossary doesn't just serve the *reader*. It serves *you*. It becomes a personal spellbook—a living, breathing record of the choices your world has made. It helps you avoid plot holes, naming inconsistencies, and conflicting backstories across books. If you're writing a Romantasy series, this is the key to keeping it all aligned.

Use ChatGPT to help with upkeep:

"Summarize these four character backstories into a clean, glossary-style format for internal use."

"List all the terms I've invented so far and suggest clearer or more poetic alternatives."

"Update the glossary entry for 'The Thorn Pact' to reflect what happens in book two."

Don't be afraid to *play* with presentation, either. A glossary can be more than a list. It can contain sketches, magical maps, family trees, spell diagrams, even dream fragments. Use ChatGPT to suggest extras:

"Design a simple spell chart for love-based magic in this Romantasy world."

"Write a poem or lullaby about the myth of the twin moons."

"Create a timeline of major romantic tragedies in the kingdom's past."

You're not just building a reference document. You're building *world texture*. Every entry, every invented term, every whispered myth is another layer in the tapestry of your story.

And when you get stuck? When you can't remember whether the capital city lies east or west, whether soul bonds fade after death, whether your magical item had three runes or four—you don't lose time or break immersion. You flip open your lorebook and step right back into the world.

That's the power of having your Romantasy world *written down, organized, and alive.*

Packaging Your Finished Romantasy for the World

You've done it. The final kiss has been written. The spell has been cast. The last page leaves your heart a little bruised in the best way. Your Romantasy story is finished—or close enough that you can finally lift your head and look around. And now the question becomes: how do you get it *out there*?

Packaging your Romantasy for the world is about more than formatting files or designing a cover—though yes, we'll get to that too. It's about stepping into a different role: from writer to storyteller, to *curator of an experience*. You're not just handing someone a book. You're inviting them into a world. The *way* you package your story sets the tone for that invitation.

Let's start with **knowing your identity**. Romantasy can lean heavily toward romance, or it can lean into fantasy with romantic elements. Your packaging—your title, your cover art, your blurb—should reflect where your story sits on that spectrum.

Ask yourself: Is your Romantasy sexy and lush? Dark and epic? Whimsical and heart-warming? A reader should be able to guess your tone from five seconds of looking at your book. That's how you attract the right audience—and avoid the dreaded "This isn't what I expected" reviews.

ChatGPT is a fantastic tool to help shape that tone. Try prompts like:

"Based on this synopsis, describe the ideal reader of this Romantasy novel."

"Write a one-line tagline that captures both the magic and the heartbreak of this love story."

"Suggest comparable books that readers of this story might also enjoy."

Next, let's talk **titles**. A good Romantasy title does one of three things: it evokes magic, it teases romance, or it hints at myth. Ideally? It does all three. Think about titles like *A Court of Thorns and Roses* or *Daughter of the Moon Goddess*. There's rhythm. There's mystery. There's a clear promise.

Ask ChatGPT:

"Give me ten Romantasy title ideas based on a story about a healer who falls for a cursed prince."

"Rewrite this title to sound more romantic and fantastical."

"Suggest a subtitle that would make this book part of a larger Romantasy series."

From there, move on to your **blurb**—the short back-cover or online description that either sells the book or gets skipped over. The key here is emotional stakes, not just plot. Don't just say what happens—say what *hurts*, what tempts, what threatens. Readers want to know what they're *going to feel*.

A good blurb often includes:

- The main character's desire or struggle
- The love interest's appeal or danger
- The magical element that changes everything
- The conflict that could tear it all apart

Use ChatGPT like this:

"Write a back-cover blurb for a Romantasy where a forbidden kiss awakens a sleeping kingdom."

"Make this blurb more emotionally charged—focus on the character's inner battle."

"Rewrite this summary to sound like a Romantasy novel from Sarah J. Maas's shelf."

Once you've nailed your core message, move on to **cover design.** If you're working with an artist, use references. Think about:

- Color palettes (deep purples, silvers, and blues tend to scream Romantasy)
- Symbols (moons, thorns, glowing runes, daggers, crowns)
- Whether you want people or just objects/settings on the cover
- Whether you want to signal "this is part of a series" visually

You can even use ChatGPT to brainstorm cover briefs:

"Describe a Romantasy book cover featuring a castle made of starlight and a heroine holding a broken crown."

"Suggest symbolic imagery for a Romantasy about love that defies death."

"Give me a visual style for a Romantasy novel that mixes cozy cottagecore and ancient magic."

If you're self-publishing, also consider how your cover *looks as a thumbnail.* On digital platforms like Amazon, most readers are browsing on phones or tablets. A cover that looks gorgeous full-size might fall flat when shrunk down. Make sure it's still readable and intriguing at a glance.

Now let's talk **formatting.** Whether you're releasing an ebook, a paperback, or both, the inside of your book should feel just as immersive as the outside. Choose a font that's elegant but readable. Add chapter headings that reflect your world (moons, runes, roses). Consider using symbols between scene breaks instead of plain asterisks—tiny touches make a difference.

You can ask ChatGPT for formatting inspiration too:

"What would a Romantasy chapter heading look like if styled like an ancient grimoire?"

"Suggest decorative scene break symbols for a Romantasy novel about fae and forbidden love."

"Give me poetic lines to include at the start of each chapter, pulled from in-world songs or legends."

And now—*launching.* Even if you're not ready for marketing campaigns or ads, think about your **reader's first impression.** Your book description, author bio, and even the opening line of your book matter. Readers want to trust that you'll take them on a journey worth investing in.

Consider building out:

- A one-page author site or landing page
- A list of keywords that match Romantasy searches (e.g., "slow burn fae romance," "enemies to lovers with magic")

- A short note to readers at the end of your book inviting them into the world (or into the next one)

You can also create bonus materials that make your book feel like part of something bigger:

- A glossary (see Chapter 58)
- A map
- A bonus epilogue
- A character interview or journal entry
- A downloadable printable of a romantic prophecy or magical item sketch

Ask ChatGPT:

"Write a heartfelt author note to include at the end of a Romantasy novel, thanking readers and teasing a sequel."

"Create a short prophecy poem to include as a teaser in the back of the book."

"Generate a fun character questionnaire for a Romantasy love interest that could be shared online."

At the end of the day, packaging your Romantasy for the world is about **trusting its magic**. You've built something rich, full of emotion and wonder. Now you're shaping how it *reaches people*. You don't need a massive budget or a full team. You need clarity, creativity, and consistency.

Let the world you built shine. Invite readers in with a whisper of promise and a hint of danger. Make them believe that behind your cover lies a story worth getting lost in.

Examples of Prompts for Romantasy Story Design and Structure

After all the writing, worldbuilding, kissing, spellcasting, heartbreak, soul-bonding, prophecy-twisting, and dream-weaving you've done, you're probably wondering how to do it all again—but maybe even faster and with more clarity next time. That's where the **right prompts** come in. A great prompt is like striking flint to stone. One spark, and suddenly a whole story lights up in your mind.

In this final chapter, we're giving you the *exact tools* you can use to generate a full Romantasy story—starting from nothing more than a vibe. Whether you're outlining, drafting, or rewriting, the way you prompt ChatGPT determines the richness of what you get back. It's not about asking for a story. It's about *guiding* the story to bloom.

Let's start with idea generation. You want a premise that blends love and magic, conflict and transformation. Try prompts like:

"Give me five Romantasy story ideas where love defies magical laws."

"Suggest a Romantasy plot where a forbidden romance rewrites a kingdom's history."

"Write a story concept based on the idea of a soul bond that forms too late to stop a war."

"What happens in a world where lovers are tested by a sentient forest before they can be together?"

Once you have a story idea, use prompts to expand it into a structure. Think about the emotional and magical journey. Ask:

"Break this Romantasy idea into a three-act structure with emotional beats and magical turning points."

"Outline a Romantasy plot where the couple starts as enemies but is forced into a magical bond."

"Create a story arc where the romance deepens as the characters uncover ancient magic together."

"Map the hero's journey for a Romantasy protagonist who is in denial about their feelings until it's almost too late."

From there, move into character creation. Don't just generate names and stats. Generate depth, contradictions, and chemistry. Try:

"Describe a Romantasy protagonist who is terrified of falling in love but destined to be bonded to a fae prince."

"Create a romantic lead who hides behind humor but carries a curse that prevents them from touching others."

"Invent a side character in a Romantasy world who is in love with someone they can never confess to."

"Write a tense, slow-burn scene where two characters with opposing magical powers are forced to share a moment of vulnerability."

Want to build out your world without overwhelming readers? Guide your prompts with constraints and tone:

"Create a Romantasy kingdom ruled by dreams, where love can be gifted or stolen."

"Describe a religious belief system where soulmates are chosen by celestial alignment."

"Design a magical object that bonds lovers through shared memories."

"Write the history of a city built on the ruins of a romantic betrayal."

As your story unfolds, use prompts to fuel specific scenes:

"Write a Romantasy scene where two characters almost kiss but are interrupted by a magical omen."

"Describe a final confrontation where the protagonist must choose between saving the world and saving the one they love."

"Write a quiet moment between lovers during a storm where unspoken feelings are revealed."

"Create a first kiss scene that's emotionally intimate, not just physical—set in a sacred, forgotten place."

You can also prompt for **twists, stakes, and choices**:

"What unexpected consequence might come from breaking a magical vow of love?"

"How might a love triangle be complicated by a prophecy that was misinterpreted?"

"Describe a magical trial designed to test whether two bonded souls truly love each other."

"Suggest a dark revelation that turns a Romantasy story on its head without killing the romance."

And when you're editing or stuck? Prompt for rewrites or better flow:

"Rewrite this scene to make the romantic tension more unbearable."

"Edit this paragraph to feel more like a fairy-tale dream sequence."

"Make this dialogue feel older, more poetic—like it belongs in an ancient Romantasy court."

"Add layers of emotional subtext to this moment using metaphor and weather."

You can also use story prompts to generate **series arcs** and worldbuilding across books:

"Plot a Romantasy series in five books where each book features a different magical kingdom and a different central romance, but all love stories affect the same prophecy."

"Describe how magical laws might shift in a Romantasy world over time, reflecting the changing beliefs about love."

"Create an overarching threat in a Romantasy series where love is outlawed and the act of falling in love is considered rebellion."

"Suggest how to tie together five different love stories into one final climactic Romantasy novel."

Even titles, themes, and moodboards can come from prompts:

"Give me title ideas for a Romantasy about a healer and a cursed prince who must kill each other to break a prophecy."

"Suggest theme pairings for a Romantasy—such as 'freedom vs. duty' or 'memory vs. desire.'"

"Describe the aesthetic of a Romantasy set in a moonlit underwater city."

"List poetic lines that could serve as chapter openers in a Romantasy novel."

And don't forget the *emotional prompts*—because at its heart, Romantasy is about love, loss, longing, and transformation.

Ask:

"Describe the feeling of realizing you've been in love all along, but you're too late to say it."

"What does it feel like to touch someone for the first time when you thought you'd never be allowed to?"

"Write a scene where a character is willing to forget everything they've ever known just to hold on to one person."

"Give me a metaphor for love that feels like magic—but dangerous, too."

When you use prompts like these, you're not just writing—you're *unfolding*. You're letting story and emotion meet on the page, discovering the narrative as it reveals itself to you through tone, mood, image, and conflict.

Let ChatGPT be your creative partner, your idea engine, your emotional compass. Give it your vision—and let it help you grow that vision into a full-blown story that aches, sings, and glows with enchantment.

And now you've got sixty chapters behind you, a complete Romantasy toolkit, and the knowledge that you can do this again—and again.

All you need is a spark.

Examples of Prompts for Designing Compelling Characters

In Romantasy, your characters are the spell. Sure, the world is magical, the plot is epic, the stakes are sky-high—but what makes readers *stay* is the moment a scarred warrior flinches at kindness, or a fae queen lets someone touch her hand for the first time in a hundred years. These stories thrive on emotional intimacy, vulnerability, and contradiction.

Designing compelling characters isn't about piling on magical traits or tortured backstories (though those can help). It's about creating people who feel *real*, who readers would follow into battle, into heartbreak, into the unknown. And with the right prompts, you can breathe life into your cast faster than you ever thought possible.

Let's dive into the kinds of prompts that will help you shape unforgettable Romantasy characters—from protagonists to side characters, lovers to villains, and everyone in between.

Start with the **emotional core** of your protagonist:

"Describe a Romantasy heroine who fears being loved more than being hated—and explain why."

"Invent a male protagonist who has always been told he's dangerous, but longs to be gentle."

"Write the internal monologue of a Romantasy lead during the moment they realize they're in love with someone they shouldn't be."

"Give me a character who doesn't believe in magic but falls for someone made of it."

You want complexity, not perfection. Characters in Romantasy should wrestle with contradictions. They can wield deadly power but crumble at the thought of emotional honesty. Or they might be brave in battle but terrified of touch.

Ask ChatGPT to help deepen those emotional contradictions:

"Create a Romantasy character who is powerful in magic but powerless in their personal life."

"Design a romantic lead who hides their feelings through arrogance—but it's all a cover for grief."

"Give me a character whose strength comes from a curse they secretly wish had never been broken."

"Describe a protagonist torn between saving the world and saving one person—and why that choice breaks them."

Now shift to **romantic dynamics**. It's not just who your characters are, but how they respond to each other. Prompt for tension, chemistry, and layered connection:

"Write the first meeting between two characters whose magic reacts violently when they're close."

"Describe a Romantasy couple where one sees love as duty and the other sees it as rebellion."

"Create a pair of soulmates who feel each other's emotions but don't speak the same language."

"Invent a romantic bond that strengthens through conflict—not comfort."

Remember, Romantasy is all about the *journey* between hearts. You want to show how the characters change each other.

Try these growth-centered prompts:

"How does this character's view of love evolve after watching someone sacrifice for them?"

"What emotional armor does your character wear—and who's the one person who can break through it?"

"What belief about themselves does your protagonist have to let go of in order to accept love?"

"Describe a key moment when a Romantasy hero realizes their power was never the magic—but the way someone looks at them."

Need side characters with purpose and presence? Don't settle for filler. Every supporting character should reflect, challenge, or mirror your leads.

Prompt for meaningful support casts:

"Create a best friend character who sees through the protagonist's lies—but loves them anyway."

"Design a mentor who teaches not through wisdom, but by making mistakes."

"Write a rival character who wants the same lover—but for reasons rooted in shared history."

"Describe a side character whose secret changes the entire story at a critical moment."

Now, let's talk about **villains and antagonists**. In Romantasy, the most compelling villains often reflect the darker side of love—obsession, jealousy, betrayal, loss. The villain might be someone who *once* loved. Or someone who never believed they could be loved at all.

Prompts to build emotionally charged antagonists:

"Write a Romantasy villain who was once the protagonist's lover—and still believes they belong together."

"Describe an antagonist whose quest for power is driven by a need to resurrect a lost soulmate."

"Invent a rival love interest who isn't evil, but truly believes the protagonist is meant for them."

"Create a cursed creature who destroys love wherever it grows—because they were denied it."

Even creatures and magical beings can have emotional resonance if you prompt them into depth:

"Describe a guardian made of stone who falls in love with the one person they're sworn to protect."

"Invent a shapeshifter who struggles with love because they've never had a stable form long enough to be known."

"Create a fae being who collects broken promises and falls for someone who never lies."

"Write a mermaid prince who saves a drowning enemy—not out of mercy, but because their voices sounded the same in his dreams."

Want fast tools for building a complete character quickly? Try profile prompts:

"Give me a Romantasy character with the following: elemental magic, an arranged marriage, a secret desire to escape."

"Design a Romantasy lead using this framework: 'They pretend to be ____, but in truth they are _____.'"

"Invent a character using three traits: fierce, lonely, loyal—and one magical gift that makes love harder."

"Generate a Romantasy romantic lead who has sworn an oath of celibacy but is slowly falling in love."

For ongoing character discovery, lean into journaling-style prompts or inner dialogue:

"Write a journal entry from a Romantasy hero the night before a battle, thinking about the person they love."

"Describe a dream that reveals a hidden fear about love."

"Write a letter your villain writes to someone they once loved—then tore up and never sent."

"Let your protagonist answer the question: 'What would you sacrifice to keep them safe?'"

All these prompts aren't just about shaping characters. They're about getting to the **emotional heart** of the story through the people who carry it. With compelling characters, even the simplest plot becomes breathtaking. And with flat characters, even the most elaborate world falls flat.

So use ChatGPT to explore your characters from every angle. Make them bleed. Make them laugh. Make them long for what they think they can't have.

In Romantasy, love is never easy—but that's what makes it beautiful.

Examples of Prompts for World Building in Romantasy Stories

Worldbuilding is where your Romantasy story gets its soul. It's not just about creating maps or naming cities. It's about building a world where love feels like destiny, where the setting heightens the tension, deepens the stakes, and reflects the emotional journey of your characters. Whether your romance blooms in a floating kingdom or beneath a cursed forest, the world should feel like a living, breathing force that reacts to the story.

But worldbuilding can get overwhelming fast. You have magic to invent, cultures to sketch out, histories to imply, politics to tangle, creatures to define, and customs to make up. That's where prompts come in. A well-aimed question can unlock an entire realm—and ChatGPT is your tireless worldbuilding partner, always ready to help fill in the blanks or spark new layers of depth.

Let's start with foundational prompts that help establish the **essence** of your Romantasy world:

"Describe a world where love is regulated by law—what happens when someone breaks the rules?"

"Invent a kingdom where magic is powered by emotional connection—how does that shape society and love?"

"What kind of world would exist if heartbreak created natural disasters?"

"Create a setting where each region worships a different type of love (romantic, platonic, familial, forbidden)."

These kinds of prompts don't just build geography or culture—they set up the emotional rules that will guide your story.

Now let's zoom into **magical systems**, because in Romantasy, magic often mirrors love. Ask questions that connect power to intimacy, vulnerability, and connection:

"Design a magical system where spells are cast by exchanging secrets."

"Create a love-based form of magic that grows stronger the longer a couple stays apart."

"What magical consequences exist for breaking a romantic vow?"

"Invent a tradition where soul bonds are formed through shared dreams—how does this affect courtship?"

Use these ideas to shape the atmosphere and structure of your world. Is magic feared, revered, or forbidden? Is it controlled by a council or flowing wildly through the world? Does magic bind lovers together—or tear them apart?

Next, worldbuilding through **culture and custom**. Ask about holidays, rituals, etiquette, and daily life—especially how they affect romantic connection.

"Describe a festival where people reveal their love through enchanted masks."

"Invent a courting ritual used by a magical race that finds physical touch overwhelming."

"What's considered the highest romantic gesture in a kingdom ruled by warriors?"

"Create a legend about two lovers who became constellations and what it means for people born under their stars."

Culture is a goldmine for conflict and connection. Maybe your main characters are from different backgrounds—one sees love as a public declaration, the other as a private secret. That cultural tension becomes story fuel.

Worldbuilding is also about **locations**—and Romantasy thrives on evocative, emotional places. These are settings where the romance ignites, withers, or flourishes.

Use prompts like:

"Describe a forest that reacts to the emotional states of those who enter."

"Invent a cliffside city where lovers meet on rooftops to escape matchmaking laws."

"Create a hidden temple where forgotten gods bless only doomed romances."

"What kind of castle was built by someone who never believed in love—but fell anyway?"

Make your locations more than just backdrops. Let them *feel*. Let them echo the romance.

Want to add **creatures, flora, and fauna** that feel rooted in the Romantasy tone? Ask ChatGPT for emotional resonance:

"Design a magical creature that mates for life and can sense heartbreak."

"Create a plant that blooms only when two people speak the truth of their love."

"Invent a winged species who write love letters on the wind."

"What kind of animal might bond with a person at birth, reflecting their romantic fate?"

And then there's **history and mythology**—the legends that shaped your world long before your main story began. These shape what your characters believe love means—and whether it can survive.

Try prompts like:

"Write a myth about a royal bloodline cursed to never find true love."

"Describe a historical war fought over a forbidden romance—and how it's remembered today."

"Create a prophecy that says when two soul-marked lovers unite, a new age will begin—but only if one dies."

"What ancient belief about love still lingers in the world's customs, even if people no longer believe it?"

This is where you can hide Easter eggs that echo your main characters' arcs. Maybe they're unknowingly reliving a myth. Maybe they reject a prophecy—only to fulfill it anyway.

Don't forget **languages and expressions**, especially romantic ones. Even one unique phrase can make your world feel layered.

"Invent a term in your fantasy language that means 'a love that haunts you.'"

"Write a traditional lullaby sung to children about waiting for their soul-bond."

"Describe how one culture in your world signals romantic interest without using words."

"What's the equivalent of 'I love you' in a kingdom that doesn't believe in love?"

You can also world-build through **contradiction**. Ask ChatGPT to challenge the world's logic:

"What's the biggest hypocrisy in a world that claims to worship romantic love?"

"How does this kingdom protect true love—but punish those who fall for the wrong person?"

"Who benefits from keeping lovers apart in this society—and why?"

"What sacred rule was once broken by a famous love story that changed the world?"

This gives your world moral tension and sets the stage for your protagonists to challenge the status quo.

And for big-picture planning, ask ChatGPT to help you organize what you've made:

"Help me build a world overview with political systems, religious beliefs, and cultural attitudes toward love."

"Organize my Romantasy world into five distinct regions with their own magical laws and romantic traditions."

"Turn these ten worldbuilding elements into a clean glossary or companion guide."

You can also go from **small to large**—build a single setting, then expand outward:

"Describe a Romantasy village where love is bartered like currency."

"What happens in a tavern where everyone forgets who they love when they enter—but remembers when they leave?"

"Create a traveling city that only appears for soul-marked lovers."

"What's hidden beneath the lake where lovers leap when their families forbid them?"

Each of these prompts invites you to shape a Romantasy world that doesn't just exist—it *feels*. It whispers myths. It pulses with longing. It breaks hearts and holds them.

Because in the end, your world isn't a map. It's a mirror. A magical reflection of the emotional journey your characters are on. Build it like a love letter. Layer it like a song.

Examples of Good Prompts for Romantasy Story Ideas

If worldbuilding is the soil and characters are the roots, then story ideas are the spark—the moment something begins to bloom. And in Romantasy, that spark is always a little bit emotional, a little bit magical, and a lot about two souls colliding in a world that may or may not want them to be together.

Sometimes the best way to unlock a new story is to ask the *right question*. One prompt, if phrased well, can ignite an entire novel. Whether you're chasing a new plot for a standalone or kicking off a sweeping Romantasy series, these prompts are designed to inspire stories where romance is not just a subplot—it's the heart of the epic.

Let's start with some **classic Romantasy story premise prompts**:

"Write a story where a prince falls in love with a girl who is cursed to forget him every time the sun rises."

"Invent a tale where a mortal and an immortal must pretend to be soulmates to stop a magical war."

"Describe a world where romantic feelings manifest as glowing light—and one girl's heart has never glowed."

"Create a story about a healer who's sworn never to love again... until she meets a wounded enemy prince."

These jumpstarts give you a clear romantic hook and a fantasy element that deepens the emotional stakes. But sometimes you want to twist something familiar. That's where **trope remix prompts** can really shine:

"Enemies-to-lovers... but they're magically linked and feel each other's pain."

"Fake relationship... but the charade is required by a sacred magical pact."

"Love triangle... but the third person is a prophecy that threatens to destroy the real couple."

"Second-chance romance... between reincarnated lovers who don't remember what tore them apart."

You can also prompt by **theme**. Maybe you want to explore love and sacrifice, or fate versus choice. Try:

"Write a Romantasy where the central theme is: 'Love means choosing again and again, not just once.'"

"Create a story based on the idea that 'not all soulmates are meant to stay together.'"

"Invent a romance set in a world where choosing love means giving up magic."

"What if two people fall in love, knowing that only one will survive the prophecy?"

Need a more visual approach? Prompt by **setting**. Let the world whisper the kind of love story it wants to tell:

"Set a Romantasy in a city built inside a giant dead god—where lovers whisper to bones for blessings."

"Create a love story that begins in a dream and bleeds into waking life."

"Write about two lovers from rival sky-ships who fall in love during a battle above the clouds."

"Set a romance in a library of living books, where one person finds a volume that tells the story of their future heartbreak."

Want stories to begin from an emotional state rather than an external event? Try **emotion-centered prompts**:

"Write about someone who's terrified of love because they saw it destroy their parents."

"Tell the story of a character who finally finds someone who sees their true self—but it's forbidden."

"Invent a romance where one person can hear thoughts and falls in love with someone who *thinks* in poetry."

"What happens when a character who's always been the protector finally lets someone protect them?"

Or try **conflict-first prompts** to immediately throw your lovers into chaos:

"Two people are soul-bonded... but one wants to break it, and the other doesn't."

"A magical plague forces lovers to stay apart—or risk killing each other."

"A prophecy says they must fall in love to save the kingdom... but they hate each other."

"Their love keeps them alive—but also powers the monster destroying the world."

For a more unusual approach, create stories from **metaphors** or **symbols**:

"Write a Romantasy based on the symbol of a cracked crown."

"A story where every lie turns into a visible tattoo—and a forbidden romance hides a hundred lies."

"Love blooms from a shared scar, glowing when they're near each other."

"A pendant that glows only when your true love is near... but it glows for two people."

You can also base story ideas on **roles and titles**:

"A bodyguard falls in love with the person they're sworn to protect—but that person is possessed."

"The last star priestess falls in love with a man raised to destroy her kind."

"A magical marriage is arranged between two people who have never met—but their dreams say otherwise."

"A monster hunter falls for the shapeshifter they're supposed to kill."

For **series-ready prompts**, focus on legacy, prophecy, or ancient love stories repeating themselves:

"Five couples across five books, each unlocking a part of an ancient magic—tied to a curse born of one tragic love."

"A Romantasy epic where each book follows a different type of forbidden romance across the same continent."

"A soul bond that skips every generation... until now."

"A bloodline prophecy says one royal heir will fall in love with their mortal enemy—and bring peace."

And when you want **prompt starters that can evolve in any direction**, use open-ended lines:

"What if the person you loved most was fated to forget you?"

"They say true love can't be forced. But what if the magic does it anyway?"

"A single kiss triggers a war between realms."

"She always knew her soulmate would be a monster. She just didn't expect to *want* him to be."

You can even ask ChatGPT to generate prompts based on a mood:

"Give me Romantasy prompts that feel tragic and dreamy."

"List ten Romantasy story ideas with cozy vibes but high emotional stakes."

"Write prompts that feel like moonlight, ink, and first love."

"Give me angsty Romantasy ideas with redemption arcs."

And don't forget—**your favorite existing books can inspire new prompts** too. Use them as fuel:

"Give me a story idea inspired by the emotional core of *Beauty and the Beast*, but with a new magical twist."

"Write a Romantasy prompt that feels like *Throne of Glass* meets *The Time Traveler's Wife*."

"Give me a Romantasy premise that blends *Pride and Prejudice* with fae politics."

"What would a Romantasy version of *The Hunger Games* look like—with a romantic plot at the center?"

Prompts don't just give you stories—they give you *permission*. Permission to write wild love. Messy love. Painful, healing, magical, world-shattering love.

And with each prompt, you're not starting from scratch. You're starting from *spark*.

One Day, One Book, One Magical Love Story: You Did It

Take a breath. Look at the world you've created. You did it. You built a kingdom out of words. You summoned two characters from nothing, gave them heartbeats and scars, gave them reasons to resist each other and even better reasons to fall in love. You bent magic around emotion. You made a story that lives, breathes, aches, and heals.

Maybe you wrote it in one day. Maybe it took you two. Or maybe this was your twentieth draft. It doesn't matter. You've created a Romantasy story—and that's no small thing. In fact, it might be the most powerful thing. Because you didn't just build a plot. You built a spell.

This chapter isn't about tips or prompts or plot fixes. This one's just for you. A reflection, a reminder, and a celebration of what it means to finish something—and why that feeling of "completion" doesn't mean it's over.

First, let's recognize the truth: writing a Romantasy story, even with ChatGPT at your side, takes vision. It takes emotional stamina. It takes the willingness to open yourself up to longing, to tension, to vulnerability. You wrote about love in a world where love is risky. That's not easy. That's brave.

You didn't just invent cool powers or paint a pretty map. You created *feeling*. The kind that echoes. The kind that stays with someone after they put the book down. The kind that makes a reader pause and whisper, "I wish I lived there... or knew them... or felt that."

Even if you think it's messy. Even if it's not perfect. Even if you wrote the whole thing with half an outline and too much caffeine. You still caught lightning. You still made something that didn't exist before you wrote it.

That's worth honoring.

And maybe you're asking: *What now?*

Now, you get to *revisit*. To polish. To deepen. To reread that kiss scene you wrote on impulse and realize—yes, it still makes your chest flutter. You get to cut what doesn't work and amplify what does. You get to revise not because it's broken, but because you believe it can shine even more.

Or maybe you're asking: *Was it good enough?*

And the answer is: If it made you *feel*, then yes. If you reached a point in the story where the characters stopped being characters and started feeling like people, then yes. If you laughed, ached, teared up, or sat quietly after a scene and thought, "Wow... that hit," then yes. A thousand times yes.

Romantasy isn't about literary perfection. It's about connection. Did you connect with your own story? You're already halfway to connecting with readers.

Now, you also have something even more valuable: *momentum*. You proved to yourself that you could do this. That you could take a flicker of an idea and follow it through to the end. That you could write a book in a day—or a week—or however long it takes.

And here's the best part: now that you've done it once, you can do it again. Faster. Better. Deeper. Maybe your next story will be a prequel. Or a spinoff. Or something entirely new. But it will be yours. And it will come easier, because you now know how to partner with the process instead of fighting it.

This book was about more than just storytelling—it was about learning how to use an AI tool like ChatGPT not to replace your creativity, but to amplify it. To brainstorm faster. To test new plot threads. To fix flat dialogue. To surprise you. And it worked, didn't it?

You're not dependent on it—you're *dancing* with it.

And if you've reached this point in the book, then you've gathered an entire Romantasy toolbox: character arcs, romantic tropes, fantasy mechanics, poetic language, structural guidance, emotional scaffolding, thematic layering, and dozens of worldbuilding tricks. You have *everything you need* to do this again—and again—and again.

So take a moment to thank yourself. For showing up. For dreaming out loud. For writing a story that deserves to exist. For following two characters into the wild and trusting they would lead you somewhere worth going.

If you want to take the next step and publish, you've got chapters here about packaging and positioning your book for the world. If you want to build a series, you now know how to expand a world without losing its emotional core. If you just want to bask in the glow of finishing something—do that. You earned it.

Print it out. Save it. Read it again in a week and marvel at what you made. Share it, if you're ready. Or guard it fiercely, if you're not. But never doubt for a second that this story matters. It matters because *you* gave it life.

And if anyone asks what you did today, just smile and say: "Oh, I wrote a Romantasy novel." Because you did.

One day. One book. One magical love story.

You did it.

I hope you found new and inspiring information here. If you liked this book, please leave a review where you bought it. Thank you from the author.

www.ingramcontent.com/pod-product-compliance
Lightning Source LLC
LaVergne TN
LVHW082341200926
848481LV00012B/3410